SUE HAVENS

make your own
toys

SEW SOFT
BEARS, BUNNIES,
MONKEYS,
PUPPIES,
AND MORE!

Potter
CRAFT
NEW YORK

CONTENTS

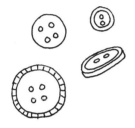

INTRODUCTION

I can't remember a time when I wasn't making things. Growing up in a remote area in upstate New York, my sister, brother, and I would pass the time "crafting." My brother would build model airplanes, and my sister and I would draw and make activity books for each other. And I was always making miniature objects for my dollhouse, including a little Monopoly board (which I still have!) and tiny framed paintings for its dining room. My dollhouse was never really about dolls, though. Animals were the main characters of my world.

Making things kept us busy. My mom taught me sewing basics early on, and I learned that I could make *anything* with whatever materials were on hand. So, starting as far back as I can remember, I was hooked on the thrill of making something that was my own, something invented, something new. Then, early in junior high school, I discovered the vast potential of vintage and recycled fabrics. After I brought home a box the size of a dishwasher full of clothing from a local church sale, my room was moved up to the attic so I'd have more space to spread out my materials and make things!

In the years since, I have experimented with making many different items—from hats, accessories, and clothing to drawings and paintings—but I always come back to sewing. I have made many mistakes along the way. I can't count how many times I have sewn the wrong sides of fabrics together, a classic and frustrating error! Mostly I can recall instances when projects just didn't turn out the way I expected, so I abandoned, changed, or tried to make the project another way. I learned much from these projects, which often became the most unexpected and inspired creations.

I also learned a lot while pursuing my formal training as an artist, particularly at the Cooper Union for the Advancement of Science and Art and in the Bard College Master of Fine Arts program. I enjoy sharing my expertise with others in many ways, whether creating things with friends and family or teaching, like my courses at Pratt Institute in New York that focus on toy-making and mastering the creation of sewn and other handmade objects. With basic sewing supplies and a few simple techniques, you can make just about anything. And this book shows you how.

Make Your Own Toys is organized in two parts. Part I explains everything you need to know to make the animals that live inside this book, from choosing fabric to using the pattern templates and assembling the toys. You also will learn the basic hand-stitches that will customize your toys. Part II presents the pattern templates, step-by-step instructions, assembly diagrams, and practical tips to make more than twenty adorable stuffed toys full of personality and wit—bunnies, bears, dogs, monkeys, and even an elephant and a penguin.

Each toy is infinitely adaptable to suit yourself, your home, or your friends. The possibilities are limitless.

HAPPY CRAFTING!

PART 1
MATERIALS, TOOLS, TECHNIQUES

As you think about making a handmade toy, ask yourself a few questions.

> What kind of toy do you want to make: a soft, slouchy, cuddly toy? an upright, stately toy? a cute—or maybe a so-ugly-it's-cute—toy? a toy with serious attitude?

> What size do you want your toy to be: pocket-sized? oversized? the perfect size to snuggle with?

> What colors, patterns, and textures do you like: bright, bold, and bumpy-textured? subdued, subtle, and soft? fluorescent and fuzzy?

Your answers will provide the basic framework for your project and help you decide which supplies to choose.

As with any craft-making, keep an open mind as you work. Sometimes a toy seems to spring fully formed from an idea that I have in my head, but most often, I modify my plans as the toy develops. I may decide at the very end to change buttons, or that the position of the ears or legs should be adjusted, or the shape of the head or body slightly altered. Be open to happy accidents and make adjustments along the way; the most interesting toys often are born of "mistakes."

My favorite part of making toys is at the very end, when the hard work (sewing the whole toy) is done, and I can think about what I want them to look like, making their expressions by choosing eyes and mouth shapes.

When designing and sewing toys, I keep things simple. Use the tools, tips, and techniques in this section to guide you in choosing fabric, cutting patterns, and making toys that are uniquely yours.

fabric

For me, toy-making begins with the thrill of the hunt. I never know what fabric I may stumble upon—some interesting little piece of rare printed fabric may trigger an idea for a toy. Finding fabrics is one of the most fun parts of toy-making; at this stage, you can imagine anything!

Look through your closet for clothes that you love but never wear, or browse the racks of your local thrift store. Because toys do not require large amounts of fabric, inexpensive (or free) fabrics lend themselves easily to toy-making. That gingham check might have been a man's dress shirt, and that brown nubby wool might have been a woman's skirt. I love thrift shops for the dizzying array of fabric textures, hues, and weights. The clothes are inexpensive (especially on discount days), and I usually can find everything I need in just one shop—from polka dots, stripes, plaids, checks, and other fun patterns to any color in the rainbow. In fact, most thrift stores arrange their clothing by color, making it easy for you to find the colors you need. Once you start looking with toy-making eyes, you will begin to see the rows of clothes as yards and yards of raw material. All you have to do is choose your favorites! Of course, you also can buy new fabrics at a store. If you do, remember to preshrink new fabric by washing before cutting your pattern pieces.

It is not important that you become an expert on fabric types, but it is important that you get a feel for different fabrics and what it is like to work with them. Avoid blouses or other garments made of sheer, silky fabrics; their slippery surfaces make measuring, cutting, and sewing difficult; contribute to weak seams; and often cause the raw edges of the fabric to unravel. Cotton fabrics and sweaters are great for making toys; spandex and other high-stretch fabrics can be difficult to work with.

tip

I always wash fabric, whether secondhand or new, right when I get home so that it is ready for cutting whenever I get inspired to craft. It's important to prewash new fabric before sewing, in case the fabric shrinks or the colors bleed. Cotton and acrylic sweaters can be machine-washed and tumbled dry. But with wool or cashmere sweaters, I recommend hand-washing and hanging the garment over a shower rod or laying it out flat on a towel to dry. But you can also experiment with shrinking wool sweaters in the dryer to get a dense, felted fabric. Before using any fabric, iron it well to remove wrinkles, creases, and folds.

As you pick materials for a toy, choose fabrics that are compatible in weight. Careful consideration to weight now will make for a better-shaped toy later. The fabrics from a thick sweater and a thin polyester shirt will stretch differently when sewn and stuffed, and a toy that combines the two fabrics may be misshapen.

If you feel unsure about the beauty of your stitching, start by using sweaters that have roughly the same stitch size and weight. It is easy to hide your seams in the bulk of the knit, and your needle will slide through without much pressure, so it's easy to attach arms and legs. Projects using sweater fabrics, like the Panda (page 24), are good beginner projects for these reasons. If you'd like to show off your stitchwork, consider using men's dress shirts, which come in every conceivable color and are great fabrics to work with. Toys made from this type of garment will likely have more structure than those made from knitwear.

Toy Safety Handmade toys are only as sturdy and safe as the materials chosen and the skill used to bind those materials together. Inevitably, a seam may tear, or a button might come off. If the toys are going to be given to a young child—which should be done at your own risk—take extra care to reinforce seams, use nontoxic fabric, and stuff the toys with hypoallergenic washable polyester fiberfill. For young children, never use weighted filler (such as dried corn, peas, or rice) in toys. Also avoid using glue, buttons, and other hard attachments in favor of hand-sewn detailing. If you need to wash a toy, place it in a mesh bag (such as those used for delicates) before machine laundering. (Note: If you use a cotton filler or weighted filler, the toy should be spot-washed by hand with a little soap and water.)

sewing supplies

You will need the following tools to make the projects in this book.

- **sewing machine (optional)** To save a lot of time and to assure that you have even, strong stitches, I highly recommend using a machine to sew together the parts of a toy before assembly. However, you can hand-stitch the parts of a toy if you like.

- **scissors** Use standard soft-grip scissors, found at sewing stores, for cutting fabric and patterns. Additionally, a pair of small (6" [15cm] or less), very sharp scissors can be helpful when making adjustments to your toy-snipping seams, notching corners, and cutting hard-to-reach areas of stitching. I use my little scissors every time I sew, sometimes in place of the seam ripper! Save your small scissors for cutting fabric; it's best to use a different pair for cutting out paper patterns.

- **ruler** Any small 6"-12" (15cm-30.5cm) plastic ruler or tape measure will do.

- **fabric marker** Fabric markers are not necessary for small toy projects, but many people find them helpful for tracing the edges of the paper patterns onto fabric or marking a template's X points onto the fabric's right side (an "X" appears on the pattern templates to indicate where the parts of a toy should align). You also could use a regular marker or fabric chalk marker. Of course, toy-making doesn't have to be an exact science, and some fabrics are difficult to mark onto anyway, so feel free to refer back to the pattern for reference and just eyeball the X-point locations as you work.

- **pins** Although I rarely use straight pins, you may find them useful for attaching paper patterns to fabric before cutting or for pinning double layers of fabric together before sewing. If you use pins, keep your pins and needles in a pincushion.

- **needles** Several types of hand-sewing needles are available, but the most commonly used are called sharps. They are medium in length, have a round eye for the thread, and are suitable for almost any fabric. Packs of standard assorted sharps are easy to find. Use a needle that slips easily through your fabric.

Embroidery needles are perfect for embellishing toys and have longer eyes to accommodate thick embroidery thread. A fine needle with a sharp point will work best. Match the needle to your thread size; the needle should be only slightly thicker at the eye than the thickness of your thread, making a hole in the fabric that the thread can pass through easily.

• **thread** The toys in this book are made with standard cotton and polyester threads. I like using neutral grey or tan thread for most projects because they work with a range of fabric colors, but a brightly colored thread can add decorative contrast to a toy if desired. If you are starting out and want to make sure your stitches appear as invisible as possible, use a thread that matches your fabric.

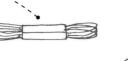

Embroidery thread is best for stitching mouths, decorative details, and other embellishments and should be used with embroidery needles. If a six-strand embroidery thread creates bulkier stitches than you would like, separate it into two- or three-strand groupings for a smooth, visible stitch.

• **seam ripper** This tool is useful for undoing stitches and opening seams.

• **iron** Before beginning any project, use an iron to press clothing and fabric scraps. In many cases, you will not need to iron as you go because stuffing a toy will smooth out wrinkles and seams. However, in some cases, you may want to press large sewn pieces before assembly. A table or other stable surface (I have used my wood floor!) will suffice for small pieces, but an ironing board may be helpful for large pieces.

• **buttons** Flat buttons are used to attach limbs and for decoration. Shank buttons (which do not have holes through the main part of the button and instead are threaded through a loop on the underside) may be used as decoration, like in the Deer and its variations (page 30).

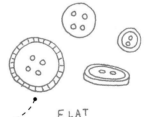

FLAT BUTTONS

SHANK BUTTONS

• **rickrack or ribbon** I use this decorative zigzag ribbon to make a hanging loop for Little Fish (page 68), but you might add other kinds of trim or ribbon to your toys.

• **multipurpose glue or cement** I use glue to attach shank buttons. It's also useful for adding thread tufts to tails, like on the Elephant (page 51), and to tack fabric pieces like patches, eye whites, or other embellishments before sewing into place.

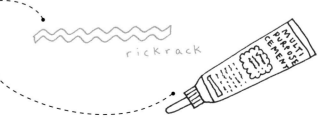

rickrack

project essentials

In this section, you will learn how to use this book to make your own toys. If you are a beginning sewer, have never made a toy before, or are just looking for a quick sewing refresher, this section will teach you more than just how to use the pattern templates (pages 76-94) in this book. You'll also learn how to prepare and cut your fabric and pick up key vocabulary and tips to help you along the way.

Each project in Part 2 includes complete written instructions with pattern templates, step-by-step assembly diagrams, and tips for choosing fabrics. Some projects also include variations that show you how to transform one kind of toy into another by changing shapes or sizes or by adding embellishments. The assembly diagrams for each project will help you quickly and easily understand how to assemble the toy and serve as a guide for attaching the parts of the toy. Red solid and dotted lines and arrows on diagrams indicate the action of the step; black dotted lines indicate edges that may be tucked under or parts that may lie behind another piece of fabric and will sometimes show the action previously performed.

Turn to page 13 for additional guidelines on my favorite techniques for toy-making and to page 19 for a guide to basic sewing stitches.

Preparing the Pattern Templates
Each pattern template is marked with a percentage according to the size at which the project was made for this book. Photocopy each template page, enlarging or reducing it by the suggested (or desired) percentage, and cut out the appropriate number of pieces as marked on the template. The resulting paper pieces will be your patterns for the project.

The percentage to enlarge the templates is only a suggestion; choose the size that suits you. **For beginners, I suggest making versions of these toys at a larger percentage,** perhaps an additional ten percent or more. This way the pieces will be easier to handle. **If you adjust the template size, make sure to adjust your fabric requirements accordingly,** because the amount of fabric called for on the corresponding project page will be for the suggested percentage.

Cutting Patterns from Fabric

With paper patterns in hand, you are ready to cut the pattern pieces from your fabric. First, take a moment to imagine how your collected fabric or clothing scraps might become part of your toy.

When making toys, you'll often cut fabric patterns in pairs, with the right sides of the fabric facing (that is, the printed "public" sides together). You will cut out your patterns from these double layers of fabric so that the right sides of the fabric are mirror images of each other, to be sewn together to form bodies, heads, and limbs. (Each pattern template notes how many fabric pieces of the particular pattern to cut out. Those marked "cut 2" or "cut 4" should be cut together in pairs.)

Wash, dry, and iron your fabric before you begin to cut. Then for patterns that require pairs of fabric for each toy part, like legs and arms, for example, match pairs of fabrics that are roughly the same size, following the fabric size guides given for each project in this book. Check that all the paper patterns for the toy you're making fit within the boundaries of your chosen fabric. Notice that some pattern pieces are labeled "cut on fold" (page 12). For these patterns, work with one large piece of fabric, folded in half.

Although I do not pin the paper patterns to my fabrics before I cut, you may prefer to do so. If pinning seems cumbersome, use a washable fabric marker (or chalk marker) in a visible color to trace your pattern directly onto the wrong side of the fabric. If you go this route, you also may want to draw *tiny* X points on the templates onto the right sides of your fabric. Keep the marks small so they aren't noticeable on the final toy. These X points are helpers to show where pieces should align.

Some of the patterns also show single black lines perpendicular to the edges, which indicate where to stop stitching and are mostly found on rounded parts. Also indicated on the templates are outlines of where muzzles, eyes, and ears are to be attached. You may wish to transfer these marks, also, to the fabric. If you choose not to mark these points onto your fabric, you'll find it helpful to have your patterns laid out in front of you for reference.

Learning the Language

Understanding some common sewing terms will help you as you make your own toys.

- **basting or tacking** A long running stitch used to hold a seam or a trim in place until it can be permanently sewn. I often baste the head of a toy to the neck opening before attaching it permanently to the body.

- **"cut on fold"** Fold a piece of fabric so that the right sides are facing each other. Place the edge of the pattern at the fold of the fabric. Cut through both folded layers of fabric around the pattern.

- **dart** Garment construction features used for shaping, typically made by sewing folds into the fabric. For example, darts are used to give the Penguin (page 58) its smooth, round head shape. You may add darts wherever you feel a shape needs to be adjusted.

- **notch** A simple snip made on the wrong side at corners between the stitching and the edge of the fabric. Notches around sharp corners help the piece turn inside out smoothly, without bunching. Make notches close to the stitch, leaving about 1/16" (1.5mm) between the seam and the cut.

- **"press flat"** Using your hand or an iron, press open the seams of two joined fabric pieces. (Pressing helps keep unruly fabric flat in preparation for the next step in sewing or assembly.)

- **"reinforce stitches at beginning and end"** When machine-sewing pieces together, **always sew extra stitches** at the beginning and ending of the seam. Simply reverse the stitch direction for several stitches (or stitch in place), then return to the forward stitch mode. Reinforcing seams in this manner helps prevent the pieces from coming apart when you turn the shapes inside out—and that can save you a lot of frustration.

- **right side** The "public" side that you want people to see. Most fabrics display the print or pattern on the right side only.

- **"right sides facing"** Position two pieces of fabric so that the right sides are facing each other. (Right sides usually should face when cutting or stitching fabric pieces.)

- **seam allowance** The distance between the edge of the fabric and the stitching. I use the edge of my sewing machine's presser foot as a guide, which is 1/4" (6mm).

- **wrong side** The "private" side of a fabric (on the inside of a garment or toy). If you use sweater fabric, the wrong side will be whichever side you do not want to see. The wrong side of most fabric does not have a print or pattern.

- **X point** Location on a pattern marked with an "X" to show where pieces or parts of a toy should match up for sewing or assembly.

Mistakes to Sew By With sewing, you can expect to make mistakes. I use my sharp small scissors all the time to correct mistakes: to adjust seams or to change the position of a button, a patch, or even a limb. (A seam ripper also could be used.) Sometimes, if part of a toy is just not lying right, I will adjust my toy with hand-stitching. No matter what happens, don't be discouraged! Some of my favorite toys have come from the most disastrous starts.

toy techniques

From cutting out the fabric patterns to sewing, stuffing, and assembling, I think you'll discover that making toys is an intuitive craft. Still, in the years I've spent making my own soft toys, I've discovered some tips and techniques that will make it easier for you to craft the most professional-looking soft toys possible. In this section, you will learn how to sew and attach all the parts that will make up your toy and how to use simple stitches to add your own finishing touches.

tip

When sewing ears or limbs with rounded corners, the smoother the arc of your sewn line, the better the finished shape.

Creating Patchwork Fabric

For some projects, such as Grande Dotted Bunny (page 65) and Graffiti Bear (page 62), you will begin by making a big piece of patchwork fabric. Then you will cut out all of the pattern pieces for your toy from this fabric. I find that T-shirts and men's dress shirts are good sources of fabric for this technique.

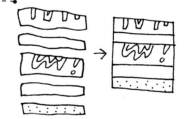

To make one large piece of fabric, start by cutting strips of the same length, approximately 1½" (3.8cm) wide. You can vary the strip widths if desired, but keep in mind that your toy shape may bow out from each seam when you stuff it. The narrower the strips, the more uniform the toy's shape will be. Stitch the strips together lengthwise as shown using a ¼" (6mm) seam allowance. When you have finished stitching, lightly press the seams flat with an iron on the cotton setting, using a piece of scrap paper or cloth between the fabric and the iron, in case the colors or designs bleed. If you're using graphic T-shirts, inked designs may melt, so work quickly!

Sewing the Parts of a Toy

I love the control and care that comes with hand-sewing. It is easy to make decisions and adjustments as I stitch. You can hand-stitch entire projects if you wish, using a running stitch at ⅛" (3mm) or smaller (page 19). However, when making the toys in this book, I suggest a combination of machine- and hand-sewing. I recommend sewing the main parts of the toy by machine, then attaching the legs, arms, body, and head (and making adjustments) by hand. Any finishing touches are best done with hand-stitching.

SMOOTH CURVES

TRIM TO
3/16"

Note: Be careful when you turn parts made from patchwork fabric right side out. Some of the joined strips may come undone if you are not careful. If this happens, repair the seams with hand-stitching.

When sewing parts of a toy together, always use a ¼" (6mm) seam allowance and sew the fabric pieces together with right sides facing, unless indicated otherwise in the project instructions. Leave a small opening through which to turn the part right side out and add stuffing. Before turning right side out, I check the shapes to make sure that the stitches and curves are even and smooth. Then, for small toys like the Deer and its variations Fox and Poodle (page 30), I like to trim the seam allowance to ³⁄₁₆" (4.5mm) outside of the stitching line. These smaller seam allowances eliminate bulk and ensure that the fabric won't buckle when you turn a part right side out, especially around the small rounded corners of muzzles and limbs.

After stuffing, it's best to hand-stitch closed any remaining openings before attaching the parts to the body or head. I use a basic fell stitch to close most openings (page 20).

From the Inside Out After sewing fabric pieces together to form a part of a toy, you will turn that part right side out. But, with small, narrow parts, such as the tail of Hot Dog (page 41), you may have some trouble doing so. Don't despair, however, it just takes a little patience—and a few tricks of the toy-making trade.

Begin by folding the edge of the opening back and pushing a bit of fabric through with your fingers. Then, use a needle to catch some of the fabric from the inside and bring it through the opening. When you have turned the fabric almost completely right side out, use a stuffing tool like a pencil or pen to push the final portion of the fabric through the opening.

Putting a Toy Together

You'll need to know a few things about assembling
your toy. This section gives you information and
options for piecing together the various parts of
your toy.

Limbs

So much of what make a toy special are the
little shifts and changes in the positioning of
arms and legs. A lot of my toy-making happens
by eyeballing as I go. In this book, I use two
methods of attaching limbs and tails to the toys.

flat stitch

- **flat-stitch attachment** Using a needle and
thread, hand-stitch the lengths of each flat edge
flush to the appropriate side seam of the body
using a basic fell stitch (page 20).

- **button attachment** Using a needle and thread,
hand-stitch the limb to the appropriate seam on
the toy's body, beginning from the inside center
point of the limb's X point and working back and
forth until a strong attachment has been made. To
reinforce the limb, draw a needle and embroidery
thread through the entire thickness of the limb.
Attach a button to the outside of the limb, and
bring the thread up through the button and then
back through the limb and body, hiding the end
stitch between the limb and body. Repeat several
times, wrap the thread four times around the area
of thread that has been stitched, and make a knot
to both neaten and strengthen the attachment.

button attachment

Muzzle

To attach a muzzle to your toy, carefully turn
the edges under ⅛" (3mm). Then tack (page 12)
or pin the muzzle onto the head at four points—
top, bottom, right, and left—to get the desired
position. Hand-stitch the muzzle to the head,
leaving a 1" (2.5cm) opening before snipping your
thread. Fill the muzzle with a bit of stuffing
through the opening, and stitch closed.

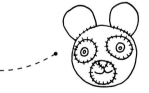

**Note: Some muzzles do not need to have the edges
tucked under. It really depends on whether you
want ragged edges or a clean, polished look.**

Ears

Before attaching ears to the body, decide whether you want to add a little stuffing, then turn the edges under ⅛" (3mm) and baste closed. Attach the ears using a fell stitch. Remember, it can be fun to play with ear placement! I've marked suggested placements on the templates, but try hand-stitching them in different places to create completely different characters. Ears can also be folded slightly in the center, before or during attachment, to change the shape.

Head

To attach a head, first use a gathering stitch (page 20) to close the head opening after stuffing, then baste (page 12) the head to the body in the desired position, centering it on the top or placing it at a slight angle. Sew around the basting stitches several times using a fell stitch (page 20) until the seam is even and the attachment is secure.

When using a gathering stitch, sometimes it makes sense to cinch the head completely closed, as when making the Lazy Kitty (page 35). However, sometimes it makes more sense to cinch closed the head opening just so the edges are drawn inward, forming an O-shape. This action hides the edges of the head before it is sewn onto the body.

baste   fell stitch

s t u f f i n g   a   t o y

Stuffing defines a toy. Many types of stuffing and filler are available. I prefer an all-purpose, machine-washable synthetic stuffing such as polyester fiberfill. (Cotton stuffing is also available, but you'll have to spot-clean a toy filled with this type.) You can add a lot of stuffing to make your toy stiff and structured, or stuff loosely to leave it floppy. The look of the body and the expression on the face will change according to how much stuffing you use. A firmly stuffed toy will have smooth curves, few puckers, and a nice overall shape.

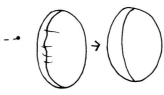

MORE STUFFING

When stuffing a toy made from patchwork fabric, take care to distribute the stuffing evenly so that you don't get a bubbly effect, especially with knitted fabrics or wide strips.

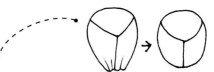

I recommend filling heads with extra stuffing to make them nice, firm, and rounded and to smooth out any wrinkles at the seams.

Most ears and muzzles are better off lightly stuffed.

When I want a toy to sit up and remain balanced without much propping, I add weighted filler (such as dried peas, rice, lentils, corn, or synthetic pellets) to the base or legs. These materials add weight and a fun "bean bag" quality to any toy. The amount of weighted filler to add will vary depending on how you'd like the toy to sit: The more you add, the more heavily weighted your toy will be. Never launder a toy made with a nonsynthetic dried filler. If you think your toy will need washing at some point in its life, synthetic pellets are the way to go.

I suggest using a paper funnel to add weighted filler. Follow the diagram below to make a simple funnel using paper and tape.

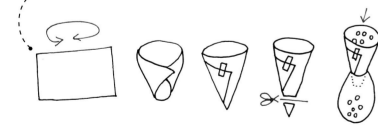

Toy Balance When you are finished sewing the main parts of the toy together, check your toy for balance—it may need some adjustment. Sometimes the head is top-heavy, or the toy doesn't sit up the way you would like. To anchor your toy, add weighted filler to the body by reopening a seam at the base of the toy. Or, add buttons where the legs are stitched in place to help anchor them in position and adjust the balance. You also can manipulate the position of the legs relative to the body by hand-stitching them in a better position.

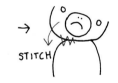

STITCH

tip

Use a stuffing tool to ease stuffing into the small areas of a toy. The eraser end of a pencil, a wooden sculpting tool, or even a big knitting needle will do the trick.

Sewing basics for toy-making

If you are new to sewing—by hand or machine—
you'll want to become familiar with some basics,
and you may want to keep your sewing machine
manual nearby. The following techniques will
be a valuable resource for you as well.

Pinning

Use pins wherever you feel they will be helpful,
whether it's pinning patterns onto fabric pieces
or pinning fabric pieces together for sewing.
Just bring each pin in and out of the fabric
at a perpendicular angle to the fabric's raw
edge. Remove pins as you get close to them in
your stitching. Do not sew over pins with your
machine.

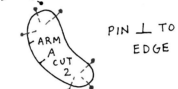

Starting and Ending Stitches

Below are a few tips that you'll need to know
in order to stitch your toy both neatly and
effectively.

- **tying a knot** Wrap the thread around your finger
twice, and roll it onto itself with your pointer
finger and thumb, pulling the thread off and away
from your finger. When I start a stitch, I look
for places where I can anchor and hide the knot
(such as between seams and behind limbs).

- **knotless start** Thread your needle with a double
strand of thread, but thread the two tails,
not the folded edge, through the eye. Take a
small stitch and bring the needle through the
stitch loop. Continue stitching as desired. This
technique is great when you can't hide a knot,
like in finishing details on a toy face.

- **no-knot glue method** For some toys, you just
can't hide the knots. In these instances, I use
a *tiny* bit of multipurpose glue to attach the end
piece to the fabric.

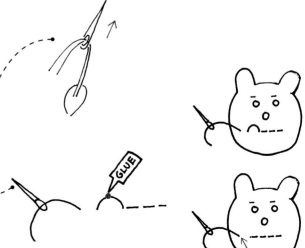

PULL THREAD SNIP HERE

- **knot behind button** Stitch into the center area behind the button several times, then end the knot as shown.

- **ending a stitch** When you have reached the last stitch, bring your needle through the area where the last stitch is located. As you pull the thread through, and before the loop of thread disappears, bring the needle through the loop and pull. Repeat for an extra secure knot.

- **burying the tails** When you are finished hand-stitching a detail, make a small knot through the end of your last stitch. Repeat, then stick the needle under and through the fabric as far as you can. The needle must be able to exit the toy. Pull on the needle and thread so that the fabric buckles a bit, and then trim the thread. When you let go, the fabric will puff back out and your thread will be hidden. I use this technique all the time to hide thread ends and conceal the end knot.

Hand-Stitching
Using hand-stitches you can create, adjust, and mend many things with a degree of control and finesse that machine-stitching can seldom match.

- **running stitch** One of the most basic stitches. Bring the needle uniformly in and out of the fabric to create stitches of equal length on both sides of the fabric. Lengthening the stitch turns it into a tacking or basting stitch, which is useful for holding two pieces of fabric together temporarily. The running stitch also can be used as a decorative surface stitch.

- **back stitch** Worked in a two steps forward, one step back fashion. The forward steps are underneath, the back step on the right side. Begin as for the running stitch. As you work subsequent stitches, bring the needle uniformly in and out of the fabric from back to front, looping each new stitch back through the entry point of the prior stitch. This stitch is good for making a solid line, like when sewing a mouth.

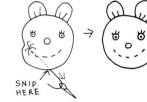

- **gathering stitch** This stitch can be used to make ruffles and more, but for the purposes of this book, I use a running stitch to gather in fabric at the base of the head of a toy. *Loosely* bring the needle uniformly in and out of the fabric as for a running stitch and then tug on the thread to tighten and gather the fabric closed.

- **fell stitch** Useful for joining two layers of fabric from the right side. Start by bringing the needle from the wrong side up to the right side of the main fabric about 1/8" (3mm) to 3/16" (4.5mm) from the fabric edge. The knot will be hidden. Insert the needle into the fabric you are attaching, directly across from its first exit point.

Take a stitch on the wrong side of the fabric, bringing the needle up through the main fabric, about 1/8" (3mm) ahead of the first exit point. Continue this step; there will be diagonal stitches on the wrong side.

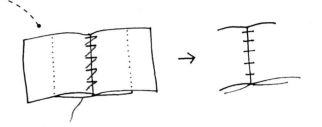

- **blanket stitch** Commonly used to decorate the edge of fabric. For example, you can see it around the edge of the Beany Bear (page 44). To make a blanket stitch, bring your knotted thread to the back side of the fabric edge, anchor the thread, and pull the needle through the fabric. Insert the needle through the fabric near the first exit point of the stitch. As you pull the thread through the fabric, slip the needle through the stitch loop you have just created. Insert the needle through the fabric near this first stitch, slipping the needle through the stitch loop as before. Repeat to continue sewing along the edge.

The key to an attractive blanket stitch is uniformity in both the depth of the stitch into the fabric and the space between stitches. When you form your last stitch, bring the needle to the back of the fabric. Knot the thread on the back of the fabric to anchor and secure the thread.

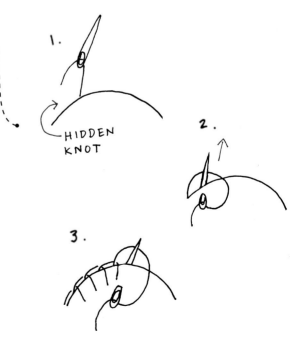

I.

HIDDEN KNOT

2.

3.

• **slip stitch** An almost invisible stitch (also known as a blind stitch) made by slipping the thread under a fold of fabric. It can be used to join two folded edges or one folded edge to a flat surface. First, fasten the thread and bring both needle and thread (use thread matching the fabric for additional invisibility) out through one folded edge of fabric. Slip the needle directly across from where it came out of the fold, through the front of the other folded fabric, drawing the thread through. Continue slipping the needle and thread through the opposing fabric edges. Pull the stitches tight so that they are invisible. End the stitch with a knot when the opening is fully closed.

This stitch is a fast and easy way to mend a seam from the right side, especially one that would be difficult to reach from the inside.

Attaching Buttons
Buttons can be used for reinforcement or as design elements.

• **flat button** Bring your needle up through the point where the button is to be placed (often indicated by an X point) and through a hole in the button, then back down through another hole in the button and back into the X point. Repeat three or four times until the button feels secure. Tie a knot behind the button, and clip the thread close to the button.

• **shank button** Make a small ⅛" (3mm) snip in the fabric where the button should be placed, apply a small amount of glue around the button shank and around the back (flat side) of the button, and press the button firmly into the hole for a few seconds to secure it. I often use shank buttons to create eyes, as for the Deer and its variations (page 30).

1.

2.

3.

4.

5.

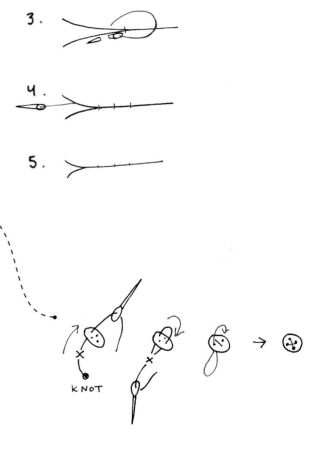

KNOT

PART II
PROJECTS

Specific instructions on how to make my favorite toys—bunnies, bears, dogs, monkeys, and even an elephant and a penguin—are provided in this section. Each project (and variations) includes pattern templates, step-by-step instructions, and assembly diagrams to guide you through the toy-making process.

As you make your own toys, I hope that you will find ways to customize the projects in this book. Of course the fabrics you choose will make your toy unique, but perhaps play around with the size of the pattern templates, attaching large limbs onto a small body, or making a toy's ears huge! Change a toy's shape by adding more or less stuffing, and go crazy with finishing—stitch on all kinds of expressions and funny faces, sew on appliqué patches or pockets, embellish seams with blanket stitch, and use buttons to add color and accent to your toy's design. Play with the process, experiment, and have fun!

panda

I wanted this bear to be instantly identifiable as a panda, so I stuck with a light-colored head, body, and muzzle, and dark-colored eye rings, limbs, and ears—just like a real panda. Using five sweaters in all, I mixed patterns within the dark colors to add texture. I even used the "wrong" side of a sweater for one of the legs!

MATERIALS

Patterns A–H (page 76)

two 12" x 14" (30.5cm x 35.5cm) light-colored sweater pieces (for head and body)

twelve 8" x 8" (20.5cm x 20.5cm) sweater pieces (for legs and ears)

one 3" x 3" (7.5cm x 7.5cm) light-colored sweater piece (for muzzle)

two 2" x 2" (5cm x 5cm) light-colored felt pieces (for eye whites)

two 4" x 4" (10cm x 10cm) dark-colored sweater pieces (for outer eyes)

one 1" x 1" (2.5cm x 2.5cm) dark-colored felt scrap (for nose)

pins and washable fabric marker, if desired

scissors

sewing needle and thread

embroidery needle and thread

two ½" (13mm) buttons (for eyes)

stuffing

INSTRUCTIONS

1   Cut out and pin the paper patterns onto the fabric, noting the number of pieces for each. Mark X points, and cut out the patterns.

2   With right sides facing, sew together the head pieces (A), leaving a 2" (5cm) opening at the neck. With right sides facing, sew together in pairs the body (B), ear (C), and leg (D) pieces, leaving openings as shown in the assembly diagrams. Turn all sewn pieces right side out at the openings, and fill with stuffing.

3   Attach the head to the body, lightly basting and then sewing around the seam again to form an even, strong attachment using a fell stitch.

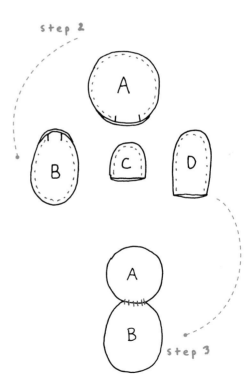

step 2

step 3

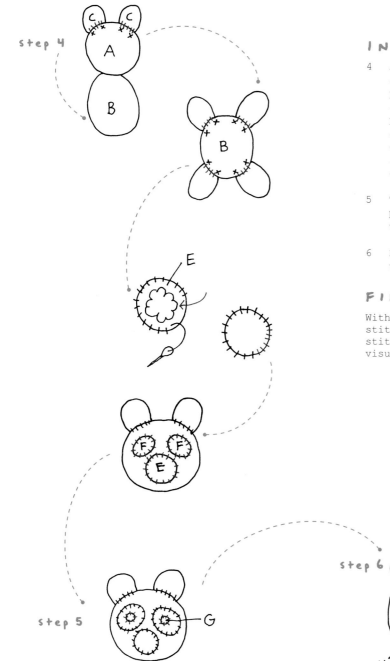

step 4

INSTRUCTIONS (cont.)

4   Attach the ears and legs using the flat-stitch
    attachment method (page 15) and the outer eye
    pieces (F) and the muzzle piece (E) to the toy
    as desired using a fell stitch, aligning X
    points and referring to the assembly diagrams
    as a guide. For the muzzle, leave a 1" (2.5cm)
    opening before you snip the thread, add some
    stuffing to the muzzle, and then stitch it
    closed as shown.

5   To complete the eyes, attach the eye white
    pieces (G) to the center of each outer eye piece
    using a fell stitch, then sew on buttons.

6   Hand-stitch the nose piece (H) onto the muzzle
    using a fell stitch.

FINISHING

With embroidery thread, stitch a mouth using a back
stitch. If the mouth is uneven or too light, back
stitch over it again to even out the line and add
visual weight.

step 5

step 6

finishing

houndstooth pup

For Houndstooth Pup, I wanted to loosely mimic a dog's coloring. This dynamic houndstooth check fabric (formerly a skirt) tied in perfectly with the color scheme as well as the idea of a "hound." The stylish pattern also suggests a fancy puppy, because fancy people wear houndstooth! The dense polyester weave works great for small projects; it holds up well and won't ravel.

MATERIALS

Patterns A–H (page 77)

two 2" x 4" (5cm x 10cm) solid fabric pieces (for outside ears)

two 12" x 12" (30.5cm x 30.5cm) patterned fabric pieces (for head, body, and inside ears)

one 2" x 2" (5cm x 5cm) white felt piece (for outer eyes)

pins and washable fabric marker, if desired

scissors

sewing needle and thread

embroidery needle and thread

two 3⁄8" (9mm) buttons (for eyes)

stuffing (and stuffing tool, if needed)

weighted filler and paper funnel

iron (if needed)

INSTRUCTIONS

1   Cut out and pin the paper patterns onto the fabric, noting the number of pieces for each. Mark X points, and cut out the patterns.

2   With right sides facing, sew together the top, front and belly of the body pieces (E) as indicated in the assembly diagram.

3   With right sides facing, place the front leg (F) between the body pieces (E), aligning X points as shown in the assembly diagram. Make sure that the edge of the front leg (F) aligns with the edge of the front body leg (E). Then, sew the lower half of the leg (F) to the front leg of the body (E) as shown.

4   Repeat step 3 with the back leg (G) and the back leg of the body (E), aligning X points and sewing the lower halves of the pieces together.

5   Repeat steps 3 and 4 to attach the remaining halves of the front and back legs to the opposite sides of each leg on the body. Sew as close to the X points as possible; you can hand-stitch the remaining open seam later with matching thread. Notch the corners of the body as shown, and trim the seam allowance to 3⁄16" (9mm). Carefully turn the body right side out at the neck opening.

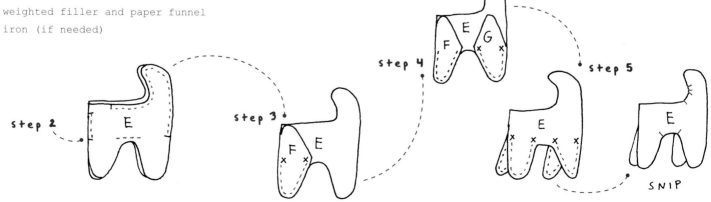

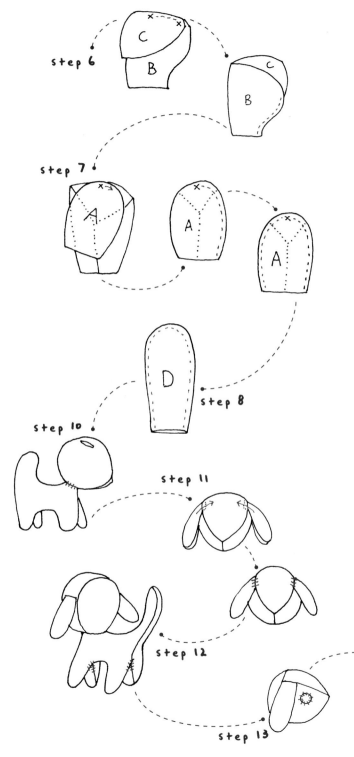

6 With right sides facing, sew the top of head (C) to a head piece (B), aligning and sewing from X point to X point from the crown to the nose as shown, leaving an opening for the ears. Then, sew the opposite edge of the top of head (C) to the remaining head piece (B). Sew closed the front edge of the 2 head pieces (B).

7 Sew the back of head piece (A) to the rest of the head. Begin sewing at the X point at the center of (C), and continue down each side of the head, leaving a neck opening as shown. Turn the head right side out at the neck opening.

8 With right sides facing, pair each solid-colored ear piece (D) with a patterned ear piece (D). Sew together the rounded edges of each pair, leaving the flat ends open.

Turn the ears right side out.

9 Fill the legs of the body with weighted filler, and fill the head and body densely with stuffing.

10 Cinch the head using a gathering stitch, and then attach the head to the body using a fell stitch.

11 Slide the ears into the open seams on the top of the head about ⅜" (9mm), making sure the solid fabric lays on the underside of the ears. Hand-stitch the seams using a slip stitch.

12 Using a slip stitch, hand-stitch closed any remaining openings at the corners of the legs.

13 Using a fell stitch, stitch on the felt eyes (H) as desired, using the assembly diagram as a guide.

FINISHING

Sew on buttons for eyes. With embroidery thread, stitch a nose and a mouth using a back stitch.

d e e r

variations: fox and poodle

When I was looking for fabric for the Deer, I found a nubby brown wool skirt with a fabric that was thick, to create a good structure, and had texture, to evoke a deer's coarse coat. When making animals, I often start by choosing fabric that resembles a characteristic of that animal, then contrast it with a fabric in a surprising color or pattern—like the green polka-dot T-shirt I used to make the deer's legs.

MATERIALS

Patterns A-D, F, G, J (pages 78-79)

two 12" x 12" (30.5cm x 30.5cm) fabric pieces (for body, legs, head, ears, and tail)

two 4" x 5" (10cm x 12.5cm) fabric pieces (for ears and head)

two 5" x 5" (12.5cm x 12.5cm) fabric pieces (for inside legs)

one 1" x 1" (2.5cm x 2.5cm) fabric piece (for nose)

pins and washable fabric marker, if desired

scissors

needle

sewing needle and thread

embroidery needle and thread

two ½" (13mm) shank buttons (for eyes)

two ¾" (2cm) flat buttons (for the legs)

stuffing and stuffing tool

multipurpose glue or cement

iron

INSTRUCTIONS

1. Cut out and pin the paper patterns onto the fabric, noting the number of pieces for each. Mark the X points, and cut out the patterns.

2. With right sides facing, sew together the inside leg pieces (D), aligning and sewing from X point to X point. Notch the corners as shown on the pattern templates. Iron flat.

3. With right sides facing, sew the inside legs (D) to the legs on the body (C), aligning X points and sewing around the rounded edges from X point to X point as shown in the assembly diagrams. Then, sew together the top seam of the body, leaving a 1½" (3.8cm) opening for the neck and an opening at the base of the legs. Trim the seam allowance at the corners to 3⁄16" (4.5mm). Turn the body right side out.

4. With right sides facing, sew the head top (B) to a head (A) piece, aligning and sewing from the center X points around the curve of the fabric as shown. Then, sew the opposite edge of the head top (B) to the remaining head (A) piece. Sew together the head with a nice, even curve from crown to chin as shown, leaving an opening at the neck. Trim the seam allowance at the nose to 3⁄16" (4.5mm). Turn the head right side out.

5. With right sides facing, sew together in pairs the ears (F), tail (G), and leg (J) pieces, leaving 1" (2.5cm) openings as shown. Trim the pointy ends of the ears and tail. Turn the ears, tail, and legs right side out using a stuffing tool.

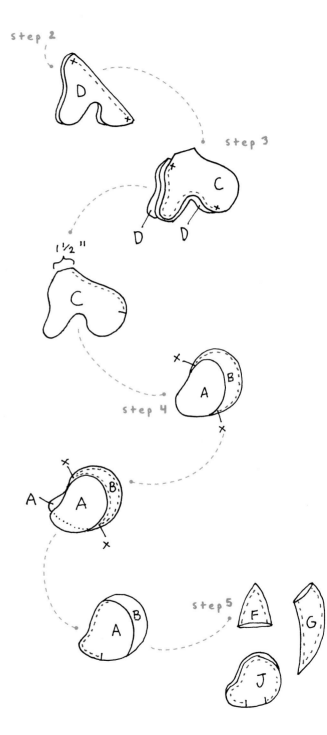

INSTRUCTIONS (cont.)

6   Fill the head and body firmly with stuffing to make nice round shapes and structure for the front legs. Use a gathering stitch to cinch the head closed. Fill the ears and tail with stuffing, and turn under the unsewn edges 3/16" (4.5mm) before hand-stitching closed using a fell stitch. Then, hand-stitch both openings on the body using a fell stitch.

7   Attach the head to the body as shown, lightly basting and then sewing around the seam again to form an even, strong attachment using a fell stitch.

8   Align the legs with the X points on the back body, and attach the legs using the button attachment method (page 15).

9   Attach the ears to the head using a fell or slip stitch, aligning X points and pinching the ears at the base as you stitch as shown.

10 Attach the tail to the body using a fell stitch, aligning X points as shown.

FINISHING

Attach the eyes using multipurpose glue (Attaching Buttons, page 21). Glue or stitch on felt or fabric for the nose, or add a button nose. With embroidery thread, hand-stitch extra detailing on the ears and body if you like.

✳ V a r i a t i o n s   Many animals can be made from the same basic body and head. To transform my Deer into a Fox and a Poodle (opposite and page 34), I changed the shapes of the ears and tails. Of course, choosing fabrics, features, and details to fit your animal can make a big difference in the look of your toy as well.

f o x

VARIATION MATERIALS

Patterns E and H (page 79) (Pattern pieces F and G are not used.)

1 patterned fabric (for tail, head, body, leg, and 2 ear pieces)

1 solid-colored fabric (for inside leg, head top, and 2 ear pieces)

2 small ½" flat (instead of shank) buttons (for eyes)

INSTRUCTIONS

1   Follow the instructions for Deer, attaching ears (E) to the head according to the assembly diagrams, with a ¼" (6mm) gap between the ears. (You will use the Fox ear pieces [E] in place of the Deer ear pieces [F].)

2   Stitch the tail to the body as for Deer. (You will use Fox tail pieces [H] in place of the Deer tail pieces [G].)

FINISHING

Sew on flat buttons for the eyes. Glue or stitch on felt or fabric for the nose, or add a button nose.

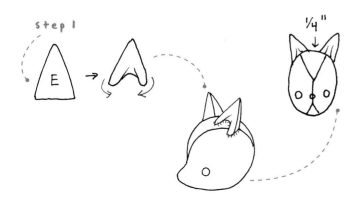

step 1

deer variation

p o o d l e

- - - - deer variation - - - -

Patterns I and K (page 79) (Pattern pieces F and G are not used.)

1 light-colored fabric (for body, head, and 2 leg pieces)

1 dark-colored fabric (for head top, inside leg, and 2 leg pieces)

1 additional fabric (for ears and tail)

7" x 2" (18cm x 5cm) fabric scrap (for tail and collar)

I N S T R U C T I O N S

1   Follow the instructions for Deer, attaching the ears (I) to the crown of the head at the seams where head (A) and head top (B) pieces meet according to the assembly diagram, using a slip stitch. (You will use the Poodle ear pieces [I] in place of the Deer ear [F] pieces.)

2   Roll up the tail piece (K) and stitch along the edge to form a tube. If you are using a striped fabric, as I did, the stripes should run across the scrap widthwise. Attach one end of the tube to the remaining (I) piece, then attach the opposite tube end to the back body at the X point that is directly above the base of the toy. (You will use tail pieces [I] and [K] in place of the Deer tail [G] pieces.)

3   As in step 2, roll up the remaining fabric scrap to form a ¼" (6mm) tube and stitch along the edge, using a fell stitch. Wrap the stitched edge of the tube facing in around Poodle's neck, and stitch the raw ends together using a fell stitch to complete the collar.

F I N I S H I N G

Attach the eyes using multipurpose glue (Attaching Buttons, page 21). Hand-stitch a nose, mouth, and eyebrows with embroidery thread using a back stitch. To neatly end your stitching, use the burying the tails or the no-knot glue method (pages 18-19).

lazy kitty

For these Lazy Kitties, I chose complementary shades of blue, gray, and green that are similar in hue and intensity. This way, each kitty reads as a unified whole. For the blue kitty, I used a favorite "spaceknit" sweater; its zigzaglike pattern reminded me of the brindled fur of many cats and dogs. The patchwork kitty sports a coat made from various T-shirt and sweater scraps.

MATERIALS

Patterns A–H (page 80)

two 12" x 18" (30.5cm x 45.5cm) fabric or patchwork pieces (for head and body, Creating Patchwork Fabric, page 13)

two 10" x 10" (25.5cm x 25.5cm) fabric pieces in complementary colors (for belly and ears)

pins and washable fabric marker, if desired

scissors

sewing needle and thread

embroidery needle and thread

two ½" (13mm) buttons (for eyes)

stuffing (and stuffing tool, if needed)

weighted filler and paper funnel

iron (if needed)

INSTRUCTIONS

1   Cut out and pin the paper patterns onto the fabric, noting the number of pieces for each. Mark X points, and cut out the patterns. Cut the ears (D) and belly (G) pieces out of a contrasting color or pattern.

2   With right sides facing, sew the head top piece (B) to a head piece (C), aligning and sewing from X point to X point from the crown to the nose, leaving an opening for the ears. Then, sew the opposite edge of the head top (B) to the remaining head piece (C). Sew closed the front edge of 2 head pieces (C).

3   Sew the back of head piece (A) to the head top (B) and side head (C) pieces. Begin sewing at the X point at the center, and continue down each side of the head, leaving a neck opening as shown. Turn the head right side out at the neck opening.

4   With right sides facing, align the X points along one side of the belly piece (G) and a body piece (H). Sew the length of the 2 pieces, from X point to X point. Repeat with the opposite side of the belly piece (G) and the remaining body piece (H). Then, sew together the 2 body pieces (H) along their unsewn edges, leaving a 2" (5cm) opening for the neck as shown. Turn the body right side out.

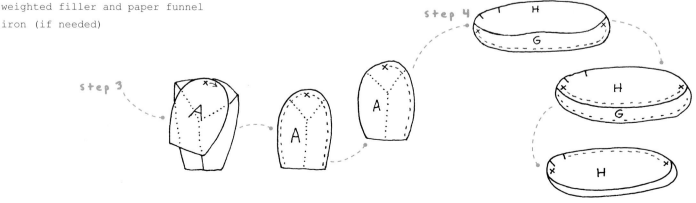

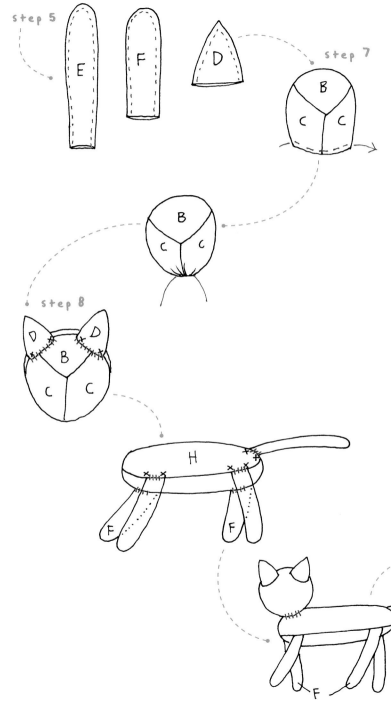

5 With right sides facing, sew together in pairs the tail (E), leg (F), and ear (D) pieces, leaving the flat ends open. Turn all pieces right side out, and fill the ears lightly with stuffing.

6 Using the funnel, fill the body one-third full with weighted filler, then with stuffing. Use the funnel to fill legs with a small amount of weighted filler, about 1 tablespoon (15mL) each.

7 Fill the head firmly with stuffing, then cinch closed the base of the head using a gathering stitch.

8 Aligning X points, attach the ears to the head and the legs and tail to the body using the flat-stitch attachment method (page 15). Attach the head to the body as shown, lightly basting and then sewing around the seam again to form an even, strong attachment using a slip stitch. The head will flop around; this kitty is very lazy!

FINISHING

Sew on buttons for eyes. With embroidery thread, stitch the mouth using a back stitch. To neatly end your stitching, use the burying the tails or the no-knot glue method (pages 18-19).

Add a felt nose, or button nose, as you like.

Hand-stitch details on the ears and body and stitch on fabric patches using a fell stitch, if desired.

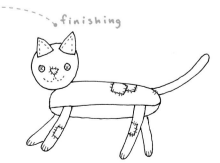

striped monkey

Striped Monkey appears to be smartly dressed in his stripy best. I used a soft brown sweater for the arms and head and one striped sweater sleeve to make the body and legs. Additional striped sweater and T-shirt scraps add colorful touches to the face, ears, arms, and legs.

MATERIALS

Patterns A-K (page 81)

two 6" x 14" (15cm x 35.5cm) fabric pieces (for body)

two 6" x 14" (15cm x 35.5cm) fabric pieces (for head, arms, and ears)

two 4" x 12" (10cm x 30.5cm) fabric pieces (for tail and ears)

one 4" x 5" (10cm x 12.5cm) fabric piece (for face)

three 3" x 3" (7.5cm x 7.5cm) fabric pieces (for arm and leg patches)

one 2" (5cm) light-colored felt piece (for eyes)

pins and washable fabric marker, if desired

scissors

sewing needle and thread

embroidery needle and thread

two ³⁄₈" (9mm) buttons (for eyes)

two ¹⁄₂" (13mm) or larger buttons (for arms)

stuffing and stuffing tool

weighted filler and paper funnel

INSTRUCTIONS

1   Cut out and pin the paper patterns onto the fabric, noting the number of pieces for each. Mark the X points, and cut out the patterns.

2   With right sides facing, sew together the body pieces (A), leaving the flat end open as shown in the assembly diagram. Repeat to join together in pairs the arm (D), head (E), and ear (C) pieces, leaving openings as shown. Fold the tail piece (F) in half lengthwise, then sew along the curved edges, leaving the flat end open. Cut notches where the legs meet the body as indicated on the template.

3   Turn all sewn pieces inside out, and fill all the parts except the tail evenly with stuffing. Fill the tail halfway with weighted filler.

4   Hand-stitch closed the ears, arms, head, and tail using a fell stitch. Cinch the body closed using a gathering stitch.

5   Attach the head to the body, lightly basting and then sewing around the seam again to form an even, strong attachment using a slip stitch.

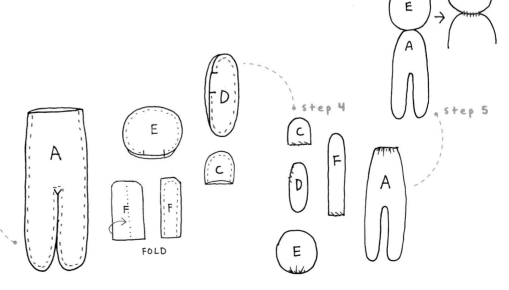

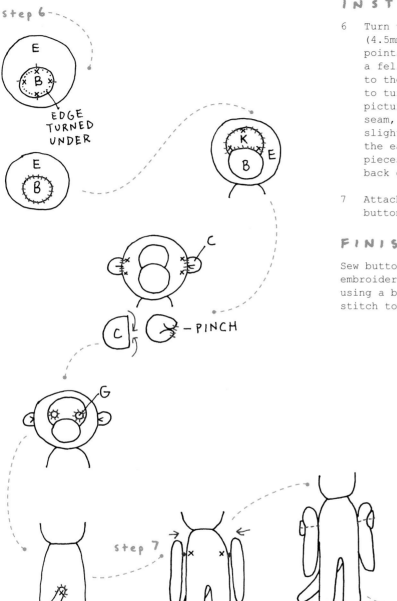

step 6

E
B
EDGE
TURNED
UNDER

E
B

K
B E

C

C — PINCH

G

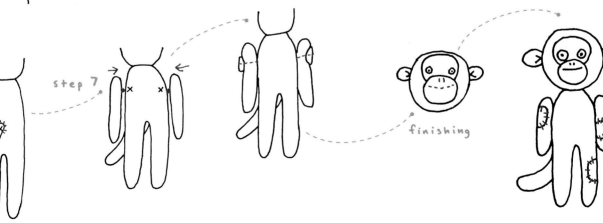

step 7

finishing

INSTRUCTIONS (cont.)

6   Turn under the edges of the muzzle piece (B) ³⁄₁₆"
(4.5mm) and tack it onto the head, aligning X
points, then stitch around the entire seam with
a fell stitch. Attach the forehead piece (K)
to the head in the same way, choosing whether
to turn under the edges or leave them raw, as
pictured. Tack the ears (C) to the head at the
seam, aligning X points and pinching the ears
slightly in the center to make a crease. Attach
the ears using a slip stitch. Attach the eye
pieces (G) to the forehead and the tail to the
back of the body using a fell stitch.

7   Attach arms to the body at X points, using the
button attachment method (page 15).

FINISHING

Sew buttons on top of each eye piece. With
embroidery thread, hand-stitch a mouth and nostrils
using a back stitch. If desired, use a blanket
stitch to attach patches with standard thread.

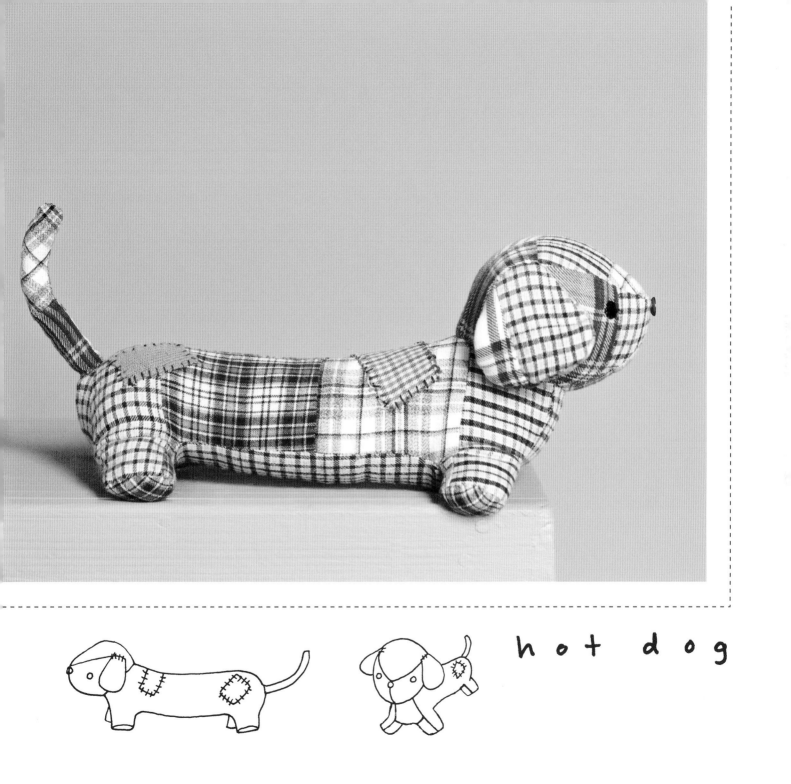

hot dog

h o t   d o g

For Hot Dog, I created a large patchwork fabric from several soft flannel men's shirts, all pleasing plaids in shades of blue, brown, and white. Because all of the pattern pieces are cut from this one patchwork fabric, Hot Dog reads as a unified whole whose funny long shape is emphasized.

MATERIALS

Patterns A–I (page 82)

one 12" x 35" (30.5cm x 90cm) patchwork fabric piece (for all parts, Creating Patchwork Fabric, page 13)

pins and washable fabric marker, if desired

scissors

sewing needle and thread

embroidery needle and thread

three ⅜" (9mm) buttons (for eyes and nose)

stuffing and stuffing tool

iron

INSTRUCTIONS

1   Fold the fabric lengthwise with right sides facing, then cut out and pin the paper patterns onto the fabric, noting the number of pieces for each. Mark the X points, and cut out the patterns. Snip along the cut lines on the belly piece (A) as marked on the pattern.

2   With right sides facing, sew together in pairs the ear (E) and tail (F) pieces, leaving the flat ends open. Begin sewing the tail at the marked line as shown in the assembly diagram. Trim the seam allowance to ³⁄₁₆" (4.5mm) and turn right side out. Fill with stuffing.

3   With right sides facing, sew the inside legs (H) to the belly (A), aligning X points as shown. Press legs flat with an iron. Fold the belly in half lengthwise, with right sides facing, and sew a ³⁄₁₆" (4.5mm) seam as shown, using a small hand- or machine-stitch. Press flat with an iron.

4   With right sides facing, sew the body pieces (G) together along the top seam only, from X point to X point as shown.

5   With right sides facing, lay the legs-belly piece (H/A) over the body, aligning X points, and sew each side closed as shown, from X point to X point.

6   Sew closed the inner edge of each leg, connecting the leg seams of the legs-belly piece to the leg seams of the body (G) pieces. Then sew closed the outer edges of the legs, connecting the outer seams of the legs-belly to the outer seams of the body as shown.

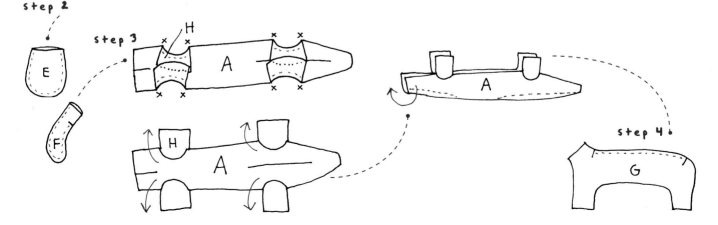

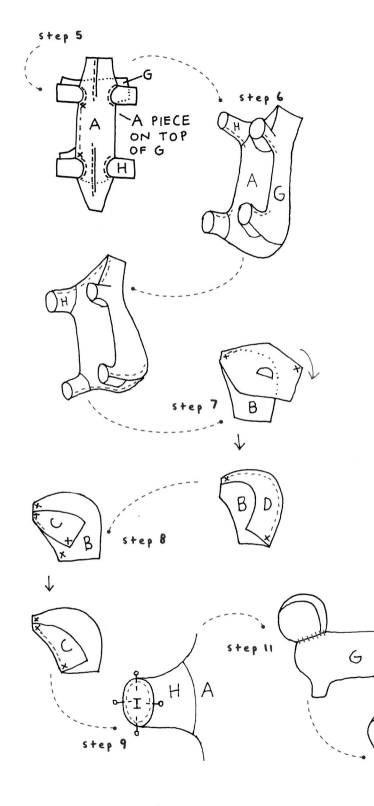

7   With right sides facing, sew the head top
    piece (D) to one head piece (B), aligning and
    sewing from X point to X point from the base of
    the head to the nose as shown. Then, sew the
    opposite edge of the head top piece (D) to the
    remaining head piece (B).

8   With right sides facing, sew one side of the
    chin piece (C) to the head, aligning X points.
    Then, sew together the opposite edges of the
    chin and head. Turn the head inside out at the
    neck opening, and fill firmly with stuffing. Use
    a gathering stitch to cinch closed the base of
    the head.

9   With right sides facing, pin and sew each sole
    piece (I) to a leg end as shown. The sole pieces
    are small, so work slowly and carefully using
    short machine stitches, about 6-7 per inch.
    If you prefer to hand-stitch, pinch the edges
    together as you sew a small running stitch, and
    carefully work around the circle.

10 Turn the body inside out at the neck opening.
    Fill the body and legs firmly with stuffing. Fill
    the tail with stuffing, using a stuffing tool.

11 Attach the head to the body as shown, lightly
    basting and then sewing around the seam again
    to form an even, strong attachment using a slip
    stitch. Then attach the ears to the head along
    its seam using a slip stitch, and attach the
    tail to the body using a fell stitch, aligning X
    points as shown.

FINISHING

Sew on buttons for the eyes and nose, or use
embroidery thread to hand-stitch these features.
With embroidery thread, hand-stitch any extra
details and stitch on patches as desired using a
fell stitch.

b e a n y   b e a r

variations: squirrel and floppy bunny

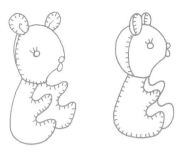

I designed Beany Bear based on my first and favorite bear, Beany, who I still have. I used a men's striped dress shirt for the fabric to add structure and added weighted filler, which makes Beany Bear a lot of fun to play with because it feels weighted in your hand like a little bean bag!

MATERIALS

Patterns A–D, F, H (pages 83–84)

two 10" x 12" (25.5cm x 30.5cm) fabric pieces (for head and body)

one 1" (2.5cm) piece of red felt (for tongue)

pins and washable fabric marker, if desired

scissors

sewing needle and thread

embroidery needle and thread

two ½" (13mm) black shank buttons (for eyes)

one ¼"–⅜" (6mm–9mm) yellow flat button (for nose)

stuffing

weighted filler and paper funnel

multipurpose glue or cement

iron

INSTRUCTIONS

1   Cut out and pin the paper patterns onto the fabric, noting the number of pieces for each. Mark the X points, and cut out the patterns.

2   With right sides facing, sew together the 2 legs/belly pieces (B), aligning and sewing from X point to X point.

3   With right sides facing, sew the legs/belly pieces (B) to the corresponding legs on the body pieces (A), aligning X points and sewing around the rounded edges from X point to X point as shown. Then, sew together the back edge of the body, leaving a 1½" (3.8cm) opening for the neck as shown. Trim the seam allowance to ³⁄₁₆" (4.5mm), and notch corners where indicated on the templates. Turn the body right side out.

4   With right sides facing, sew the head top piece (D) to a head piece (C), aligning X points and sewing from crown to nose as shown. Then, sew the opposite edge of the head top piece (D) to the remaining head piece (C). Sew together the front edge of the head pieces (C) from nose to neck as shown. Trim the seam allowance at the nose to ³⁄₁₆" (4.5mm). Turn the head right side out.

5   With right sides facing, sew together the ear pieces (F), leaving the flat end open. Turn the ears right side out. Fill the body first with ½ cup weighted filler, then continue to fill firmly with stuffing to make nice round shapes and structure. Fill the ears and head with stuffing. Then, baste all openings closed. As you baste the ears, turn under the fabric edges ³⁄₁₆" (4.5mm).

6   Cinch the head closed using a gathering stitch. Attach the head to the body, lightly basting and then sewing around the seam again using a slip stitch.

7   Attach the ears to the head using a slip stitch, aligning X points and pinching the ears in half as you stitch to form a U-shape as shown.

FINISHING

Attach the shank buttons as eyes using multipurpose glue (Attaching Buttons, page 21). Glue or sew on a button nose and felt tongue (H) as shown. With embroidery thread, embellish the seams of your bear using a blanket stitch (page 20).

* Variations   Fabric choice is a great way to transform one animal into another. For Squirrel (page 46) I chose a patterned thick wool skirt to accentuate his shape, including his prominent tail. Fabric with a lot of softness and give, like the cashmere sweater used for Floppy Bunny (page 47), gives the toy a completely different look, even though it uses the same head and body.

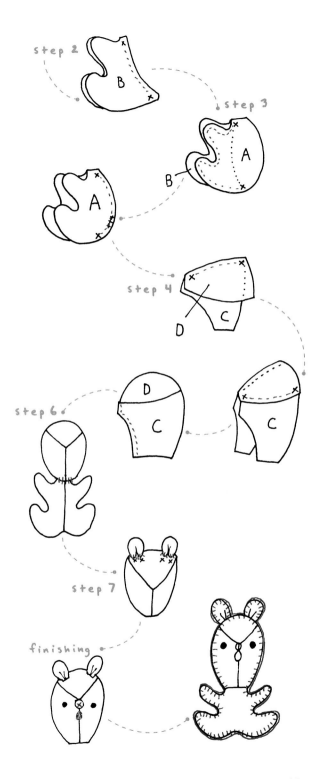

step 2

step 3

step 4

step 6

step 7

finishing

squirrel

----- beany bear variation -----

VARIATION MATERIALS

Patterns G, I-J (pages 83-84) (Pattern piece H is not used.)

2 colors of fabric, or 1 solid fabric (for legs/belly and 2 ear pieces) and 1 patterned fabric (for body, tail, and 2 ear pieces)

one 2" x 2" (5cm x 5cm) scrap of gray or white felt (for eyes)

1 small fabric scrap (for nose)

two ½" (13mm) flat (instead of shank) buttons (for eyes)

embroidery needle and thread

INSTRUCTIONS

1   Follow the instructions for Beany Bear, filling the body with ½ cup (118mL) weighted filler if desired.

2   With right sides facing, sew together the rounded edges of the tail pieces (G). Turn the tail right side out, stuff, and stitch the opening closed using a fell stitch. Attach the tail to the body along the tail's front seam, aligning X points as shown.

3   Attach the felt eye pieces (I) with a fell stitch, then sew buttons on top, as indicated on the pattern. Sew on the nose (J) with standard thread at the intersection of all the head pieces.

FINISHING

Hand-stitch a mouth with embroidery thread using a back stitch. Use the burying the tails method or the no-knot glue method to neatly end your stitches (pages 18-19).

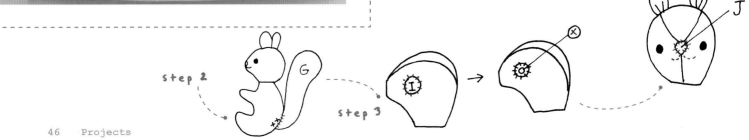

floppy bunny

beany bear variation

VARIATION MATERIALS

Pattern E (page 83) (Pattern pieces F-J are not used.)

1 soft fabric like a cashmere knit (for body, head, head top, and 2 ear pieces)

1 patterned fabric (for legs/belly and 2 ear pieces) (The Bunny ear pieces [J] are used in place of Beany Bear ear pieces [E].)

two ½" (13mm) shank buttons for eyes

embroidery thread

INSTRUCTIONS

1   Follow the instructions for Beany Bear, but in step 5 when sewing the ears (E), pair alternate patterns together.

2   Continue to follow the Beany Bear instructions. At step 8, stitch the ears to the seam at the head top (D), aligning X points as shown. The patterned fabric should face the front of the toy.

FINISHING

Attach the buttons as eyes using multipurpose glue (Attaching Buttons, page 21).

With embroidery thread, stitch a nose and mouth using a back stitch. Use the burying the tails or the no-knot glue method to neatly end your stitches (pages 18-19).

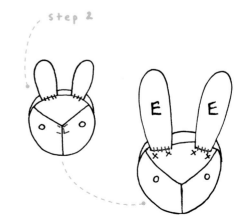

step 2

mini monkey

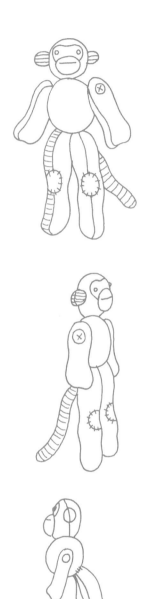

The fun in making Mini Monkey is in collecting stripes! I used ten fabrics from striped sweaters and T-shirts. Stack your fabrics to see how they'll look together and to help you choose which to combine. When you put them all together, your monkey will dance with pattern and color.

INSTRUCTIONS

1   Cut out and pin the paper patterns onto the fabric, noting the number of pieces for each. Mark X points, and cut out the patterns.

2   With right sides facing, sew together the body pieces (A), leaving an opening of about 1¼" (3cm) at the neck as shown in the assembly diagram. Repeat to join together in pairs the head (B), tail (F), arm (G), leg (H), and ear (E) pieces, leaving openings as shown. Trim the seam allowance for all pieces to ³⁄₁₆" (4.5mm), and turn right side out.

3   Fill the body and the tail halfway with weighted filler. Fill the body, head, arms, legs, and ears with stuffing, but do not add stuffing to the tail. Hand-stitch closed all pieces as shown using a small fell stitch or slip stitch.

4   Attach the head to the body as shown, lightly basting and then sewing around the seam again to form an even, strong attachment using a fell stitch.

MATERIALS

Patterns A–I (page 85)

fifteen to twenty 5" x 10" (12.5cm x 25.5cm) fabric pieces

pins and washable fabric marker, if desired

scissors

sewing needle and thread

embroidery needle and thread

two ³⁄₈" (9mm) buttons (for eyes)

two ½" (13mm) buttons (for arms)

stuffing and stuffing tool

weighted filler and paper funnel

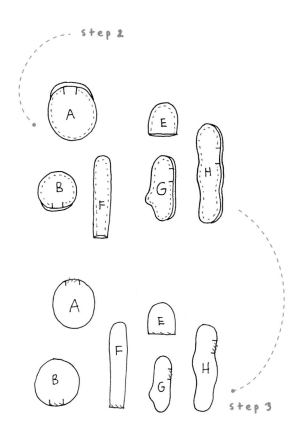

step 2

step 3

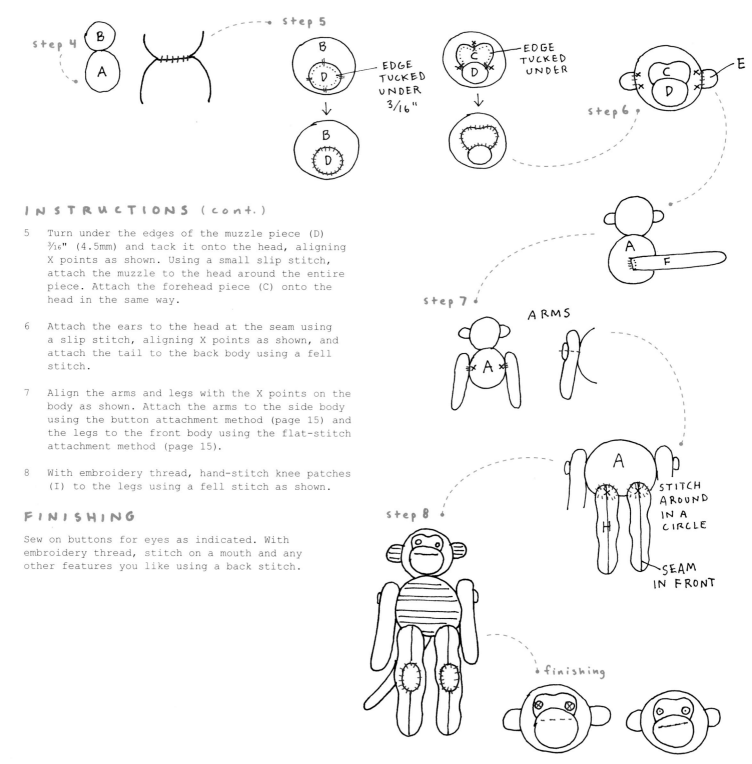

INSTRUCTIONS (cont.)

5   Turn under the edges of the muzzle piece (D)
    3/16" (4.5mm) and tack it onto the head, aligning
    X points as shown. Using a small slip stitch,
    attach the muzzle to the head around the entire
    piece. Attach the forehead piece (C) onto the
    head in the same way.

6   Attach the ears to the head at the seam using
    a slip stitch, aligning X points as shown, and
    attach the tail to the back body using a fell
    stitch.

7   Align the arms and legs with the X points on the
    body as shown. Attach the arms to the side body
    using the button attachment method (page 15) and
    the legs to the front body using the flat-stitch
    attachment method (page 15).

8   With embroidery thread, hand-stitch knee patches
    (I) to the legs using a fell stitch as shown.

FINISHING

Sew on buttons for eyes as indicated. With
embroidery thread, stitch on a mouth and any
other features you like using a back stitch.

elephant

Simplifying color can be a great way to accentuate what is interesting about a toy. In this case, I wanted to highlight the elephant's shape, so I used two gray men's shirts—one with a subtle stripe—and added final touches with patches and embroidery. The colors and tone are muted, right down to the buttons and sprightly tail.

MATERIALS

Patterns A-I (page 86)

two 20" x 20" (51cm x 51cm) fabric pieces (for body and all parts except inside ears)

two 7" x 7" (18cm x 18cm) fabric pieces (for inside ears)

three 3" x 3" (7.5cm x 7.5cm) fabric pieces (for patches)

pins and washable fabric marker, if desired

scissors

sewing needle and thread

embroidery needle and thread

6 assorted buttons (⅜" [9mm] for eyes and ¾"-1" [2cm-2.5cm] for limb attachments)

stuffing and stuffing tool

multipurpose glue (optional)

iron (if needed)

INSTRUCTIONS

1   Cut out and pin the paper patterns onto the fabric, noting the number of pieces for each. Mark the X points, and cut out the patterns. Cut out one pair of ear pieces (C) from a fabric that contrasts with the body fabric in color or pattern.

2   With right sides facing, sew together in pairs the trunk (E), ear (C), front leg (D), and back leg (F) pieces, leaving openings as shown in the assembly diagrams. When sewing the ears, pair one solid-colored piece with a patterned piece. Turn all sewn pieces right side out, and fill with stuffing using the stuffing tool. Hand-stitch closed the front and back legs and the ears as shown using a fell stitch.

3   With right sides facing, sew the body center piece (I) to one body piece (A), aligning and sewing from X point to X point around the curve of the body as shown. Then, sew the opposite side of the body center piece (I) to the remaining body piece (A).

4   Repeat step 3 to join the head center piece (H) to the head pieces (B). Turn the head and body right side out, and fill firmly with stuffing.

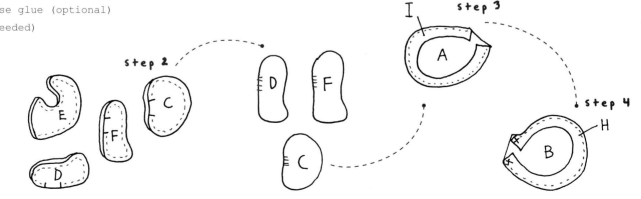

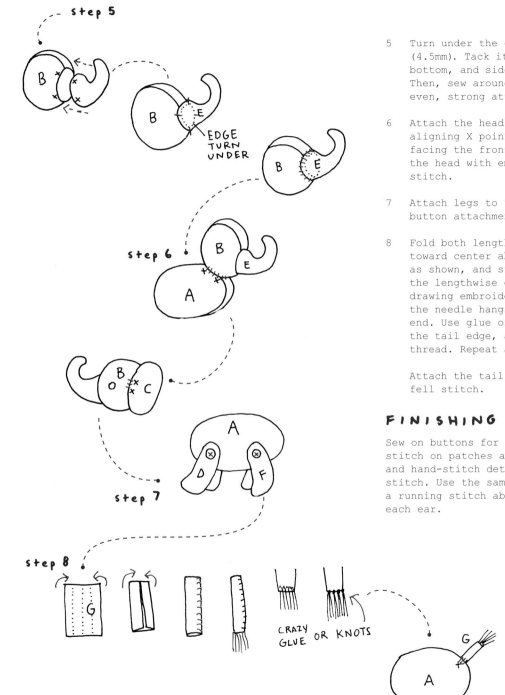

5 Turn under the edges of the trunk (E) ³⁄₁₆"
   (4.5mm). Tack it onto the head at the top,
   bottom, and sides, aligning X points as shown.
   Then, sew around the entire seam to form an
   even, strong attachment.

6 Attach the head to the body using a slip stitch,
   aligning X points. With the patterned fabric
   facing the front of the toy, attach the ears to
   the head with embroidery thread using a fell
   stitch.

7 Attach legs to the body at X points using the
   button attachment method (page 15) as shown.

8 Fold both lengthwise edges of the tail piece (G)
   toward center about ³⁄₁₆" (4.5mm). Fold once again
   as shown, and stitch the folds closed along
   the lengthwise edge. Add fringe to the tail by
   drawing embroidery thread through the edge until
   the needle hangs about 1" (2.5cm) from the tail
   end. Use glue or knots to secure thread against
   the tail edge, and snip dangling needle and
   thread. Repeat as desired across tail.

   Attach the tail to the body at X points using a
   fell stitch.

FINISHING

Sew on buttons for eyes. With embroidery thread,
stitch on patches as shown using a fell stitch,
and hand-stitch details if desired using a running
stitch. Use the same color embroidery thread to sew
a running stitch about ¼" (6mm) from the edge of
each ear.

s p a c e m a n

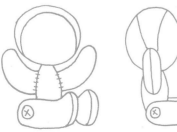

When creating a toy without facial features or other finishing embellishments, you can use a lot of colors and fabrics to add interest. I used several T-shirt scraps to make Spaceman. This toy also shows why you don't have to get frustrated by sewing "mistakes." When I accidentally sewed on this toy's head the wrong way, I discovered an unexpected new little guy.

MATERIALS

Patterns A-E (page 87)

twelve 6" x 6" (15cm x 15cm) fabric pieces (for head, body, arms, and legs)

one 7" x 12" (18cm x 30.5cm) T-shirt fabric piece (for head top)

pins and washable fabric marker, if desired

scissors

sewing needle and thread

stuffing

iron (if needed)

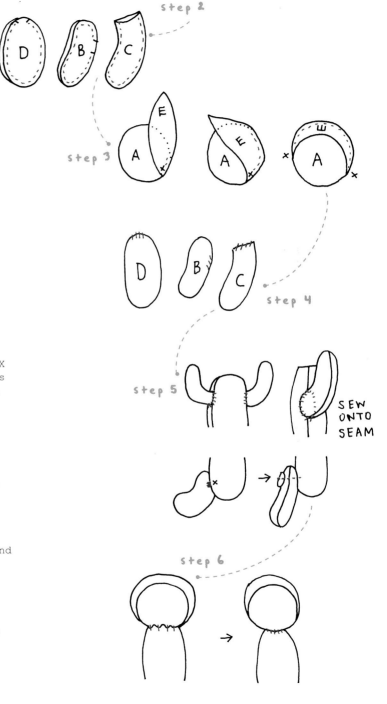

INSTRUCTIONS

1   Cut out and pin the paper patterns onto the fabric, noting the number of pieces for each. Mark the X points, and cut out the patterns.

2   With right sides facing, sew together in pairs the body (D), leg (B), and arm (C) pieces, leaving openings as shown.

3   With right sides facing, sew the head top (E) to a head (A) piece, aligning and sewing from X point to X point all the way around the head as shown. Then, sew the opposite edge of the head top piece (E) to the remaining head piece (A).

4   Turn all sewn pieces right side out and fill with stuffing. Close the leg, arm, and body openings using a small fell stitch.

5   Aligning X points, attach the arms to the side body seams using the flat-stitch attachment method, and attach the legs to the body using the button attachment method (page 15).

6   Attach the head to the body, lightly basting and then sewing around the seam again to form an even, strong attachment using a fell stitch.

✻ v a r i a t i o n s   Little Bunny and Monkey (pages 56 and 57) are just two of the many variations that you can make by adding features to the basic Spaceman. Add ears and a muzzle, hand-stitched features on the face, border stitching, appliqué patches, or other details. Use your imagination!

little bunny

VARIATION MATERIALS

Patterns F and G (page 87)

2 colors of fabric (1 for head, back, arms, and legs and 1 for face and belly)

two 6" x 6" (15cm x 15cm) pieces of gray fabric (for muzzle and 2 ear pieces)

two 4" x 4" (10cm x 10cm) pieces of plaid fabric (for 2 ear pieces)

embroidery needle and thread in 2 colors

two ½" (13mm) buttons (for eyes)

INSTRUCTIONS

1   Follow the Spaceman instructions, being sure to assemble the face and belly toward the front of the toy.

2   With right sides facing, sew the rounded edges of the ear pieces (G) together. Turn right side out, lightly stuff, and stitch the flat ends closed, pinching as you stitch to create a small crease. Attach the ears to the top of the head using a slip stitch, aligning X points as shown.

3   Turn under the edges of the muzzle piece (F) ³⁄₁₆" (4.5mm) and tack it onto the head. Attach the muzzle to the head using a small slip stitch, leaving a 1½" (3.8cm) opening as shown. Add a small amount of stuffing, and sew the opening closed with a fell stitch.

FINISHING

Sew on buttons for eyes, and stitch on a nose and mouth with embroidery thread. To neatly end your stitching, use the burying the tails or the no-knot glue method (pages 18-19).

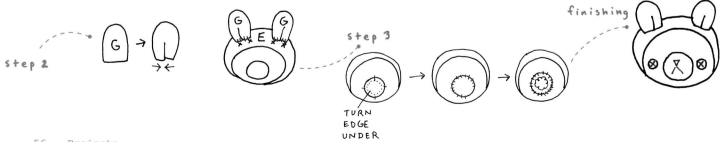

monkey

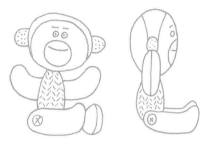

VARIATION MATERIALS

Patterns F and H (page 87) (Pattern G is not used.)

3 main fabrics (1 textured fabric for arms, legs, and head top; and 1 textured fabric for body and 2 ear pieces; and 1 additional fabric for head)

one 4" x 4" (10cm x 10cm) piece of fabric (for muzzle)

two 6" x 6" (15cm x 15cm) pieces of fabric (for 2 front ear pieces)

embroidery needle and thread

two ½" (13mm) buttons (for eyes)

INSTRUCTIONS

1   Follow the instructions for the Spaceman and the additional instructions for the Little Bunny variation.

2   When attaching the ears, simply stitch the ears to the side of the head using a slip stitch. Attach the muzzle as for the Little Bunny.

FINISHING

Use the Monkey assembly diagrams to guide eye and ear placement and to add the eyebrows and mouth using a back stitch. To neatly end your stitching, use the burying the tails or the no-knot glue method (pages 18-19).

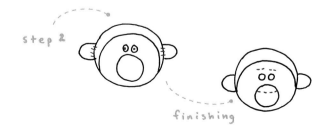

step 2

finishing

penguin

I used the fabric from two men's shirts to make my sharp-dressed Penguin. For a classic "tuxedo" look, I used one light striped fabric for the belly, sides of the head, and beak and a dark striped fabric for the rest. The crisp nature of the dress shirt fabric and firm stuffing give this toy nice structure and good posture.

MATERIALS

Patterns A-J (page 88)

two 10" x 10" (25.5cm x 25.5cm) dark-colored fabric pieces (for back body, head top, wings, tail, and feet)

one 3" x 7" (7.5cm x 18cm) light-colored fabric piece (for front body, head sides, and beak)

one 2" x 2" (5cm x 5cm) light-colored sweater scrap (for bib)

pins and washable fabric marker, if desired

scissors

sewing needle and thread

embroidery needle and thread

four ⅜" (9mm) buttons (for eyes and bib)

stuffing

weighted filler and paper funnel

iron

INSTRUCTIONS

1   Cut out and pin the paper patterns onto the fabric, noting the number of pieces for each. Mark the X points, and cut out the patterns.

2   Fold each head side piece (D) in half, right sides facing. Sew a smooth arc to create a dart as marked on the template. Lay or press flat. Repeat with the head top (B) piece, making two darts as shown in the assembly diagram. Stitch from the top of the dart to the bottom edge, creating a shallow ⅛" (3mm) seam allowance.

3   With right sides facing, sew the head top piece (B) to one head side piece (D), aligning and sewing from the center X points along each curved edge of the head side piece as shown. Then, sew the opposite edge of the head top (B) to the remaining head piece (D).

INSTRUCTIONS (cont.)

4   With right sides facing, sew the front body
    piece (A) to a body side piece (E), aligning
    and sewing from X point to X point. Then sew the
    opposite edge of the front body piece (A) to
    the remaining body side piece (E). With right
    sides facing, sew both side edges to the back
    body piece (A), aligning X points. Turn the body
    right side out.

5   With right sides facing, sew the bottom piece
    (J) onto the body as shown, aligning X points.
    Work your way around as best as you can. If
    necessary, finish any unsewn edges by turning
    the body inside out again, and hand-stitching
    to close. Turn the body right side out, and
    fill first with ⅓–½ cup (79mL–118mL) weighted
    filler, then firmly with stuffing.

6   Turn the head right side out, and fill firmly
    with stuffing. Midway through stuffing, cinch
    in the base of the head using a gathering
    stitch, but do not close the opening completely.
    Continue stuffing until firm and round.

7   Position the head over the body, tucking the
    unsewn edges under ³⁄₁₆" (4.5mm), and tack it in
    place as shown. Attach the head to the body,
    lightly basting and then sewing around the seam
    again to form an even, strong attachment using a
    fell stitch.

8   With the right sides facing, sew together two
    pairs of wing pieces (C), leaving a 2" (5cm)
    opening as shown. Trim the seam allowance to ³⁄₁₆"
    (4.5mm), and turn the wings right side out. Fill
    the wings with stuffing, and close the openings
    using a fell stitch.

9   Attach the wings to the body at slight forward
    angles, pinching the wings in half to pucker the
    fabric. Using a fell stitch, stitch along this
    edge, connecting the inside center of the wing
    to the body.

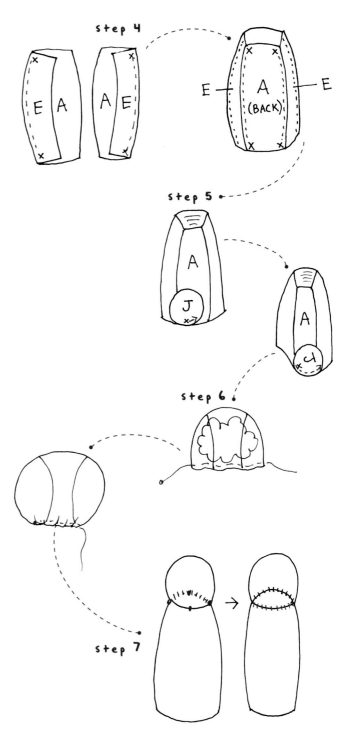

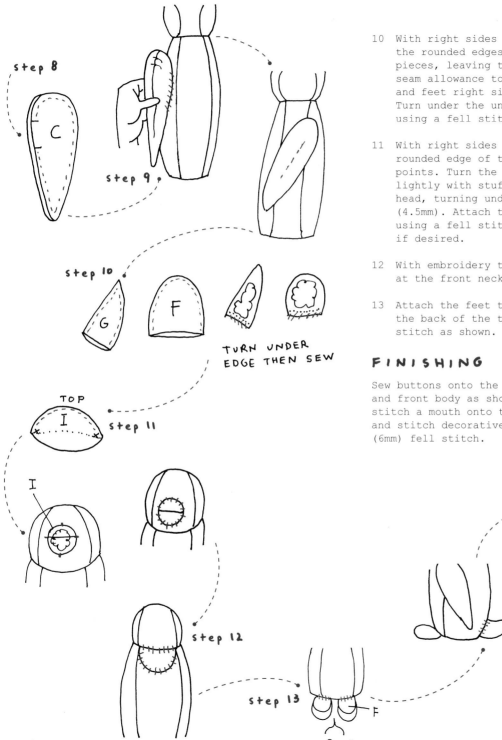

10 With right sides facing, sew together in pairs the rounded edges of the tail (G) and feet (F) pieces, leaving the flat ends open. Trim the seam allowance to $\frac{3}{16}$" (4.5mm). Turn the tail and feet right side out, and fill with stuffing. Turn under the unsewn edges, and sew closed using a fell stitch.

11 With right sides facing, sew together one rounded edge of the beak pieces (I), aligning X points. Turn the beak right side out, and fill lightly with stuffing. Then, tack it onto the head, turning under the unsewn edge about $\frac{3}{16}$" (4.5mm). Attach the beak to the head securely using a fell stitch, adding stuffing as you go if desired.

12 With embroidery thread, stitch the bib piece (H) at the front neck as shown using a fell stitch.

13 Attach the feet to the bottom and the tail to the back of the toy using a slip stitch or fell stitch as shown.

FINISHING

Sew buttons onto the head for eyes and onto the bib and front body as shown. With embroidery thread, stitch a mouth onto the beak using a back stitch, and stitch decorative edges as desired using a $\frac{1}{4}$" (6mm) fell stitch.

step 8

step 9

step 10

TURN UNDER
EDGE THEN SEW

TOP

step 11

I

step 12

step 13

3/4"

finishing

G

F

graffiti bear

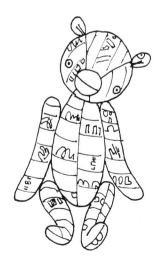

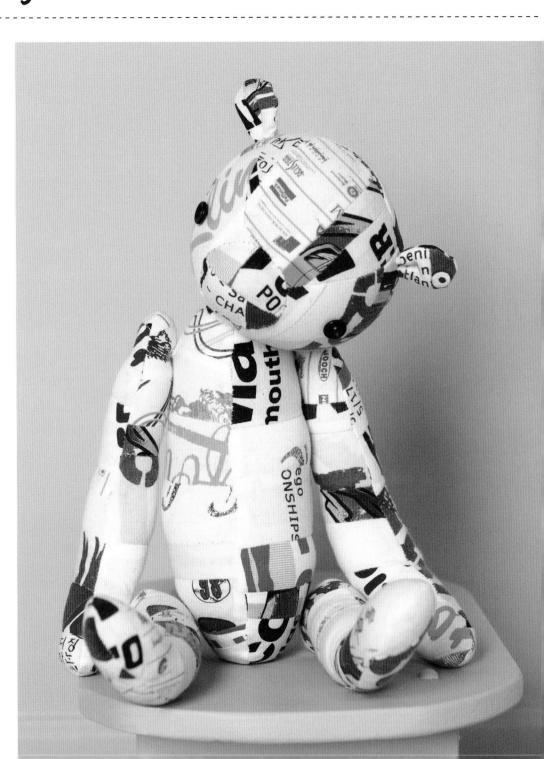

Graffiti Bear takes his name from designs and logos gathered from T-shirts. Choose T-shirts in the same color or different colors (you could make a black, white, pink, or multicolored bear!), cut strips from the printed designs, and use those strips to make a patchwork fabric.

MATERIALS

Patterns A-J (pages 89-90)

one 14" x 26" (35.5cm x 66cm) patchwork fabric piece (Creating Patchwork Fabric, page 13)

pins and washable fabric marker, if desired

scissors

sewing needle and thread

embroidery needle and thread

two ½" (13mm) buttons

stuffing

iron (if needed)

INSTRUCTIONS

1   Fold the fabric lengthwise with right sides facing, then cut out and pin the paper patterns onto the fabric, noting the number of pieces for each. Match the orientation of the patchwork strips on the paper patterns to your fabric. Mark the X points, and cut out the patterns.

2   With right sides facing, sew together in pairs the body (A), arm (C), leg (B), and ear (J) pieces, leaving openings as shown in the assembly diagrams. Carefully turn all sewn pieces right side out. Using a small fell stitch, repair any patchwork seams that have come apart (page 14).

3   With right sides facing, sew the head top (E) to one head piece (D), aligning and sewing from X point to X point from the crown to the nose as shown. Then, sew the opposite edge of the head top (E) to the remaining head piece (D).

4   With right sides facing, sew the chin piece (G) to one head piece (D) at the remaining X points as shown. Then, sew the opposite side of the chin (G) to the opposite head piece (D). Trim the seam allowance around the head to ³⁄₁₆" (4.5mm).

5   Attach the head back piece (F) to the sewn head pieces. Begin sewing at the X points in the center of the sewn head pieces, and continue down each side, leaving a neck opening as shown. Turn the head right side out.

6   Fill the head, body, arms, and legs firmly with stuffing. Add a small amount of stuffing to the ears. Stitch closed all openings using a fell stitch, and cinch closed the base of the head using a gathering stitch.

step 2

step 3

step 4

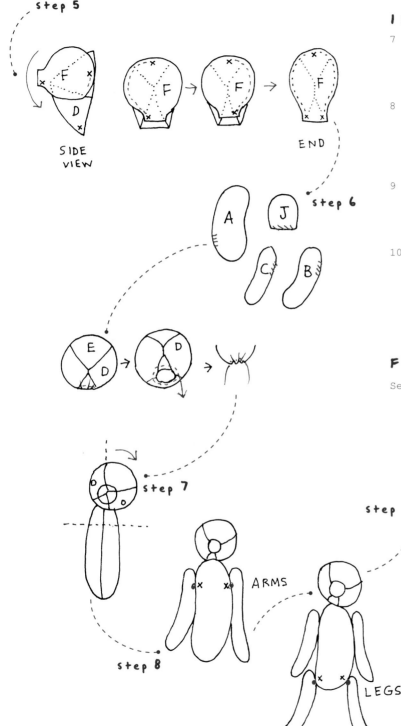

step 5

SIDE
VIEW

END

step 6

A   J

C   B

E
D   D

step 7

step 8

ARMS

LEGS

7   Attach the head to the body at a slight angle as shown, lightly basting and then sewing around the seam again to form an even, strong attachment using a slip stitch.

8   Aligning X points as shown, attach the arms and legs to the body as if using the button attachment method (page 15), but using thread only (no buttons). If desired, add buttons for reinforcement and decoration.

9   Turn under the edges of the ears, and attach the ears to the head using a slip stitch, aligning X points and pinching the ears slightly in the center as you stitch to form a U-shape.

10 With right sides facing, sew the muzzle top (H) to the muzzle bottom (I) from X point to X point as shown. Then turn under the edges of the muzzle 3/16" (4.5mm) and tack it onto the head, centering it over the convergence points of the head and chin pieces. Add stuffing and sew around the entire piece using a fell stitch.

FINISHING

Sew on buttons for eyes as indicated on the pattern.

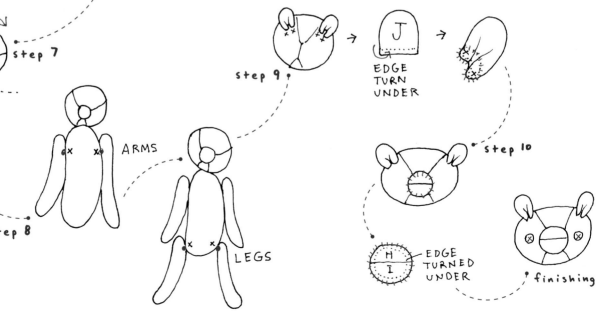

step 9

J
EDGE
TURN
UNDER

step 10

H
I
EDGE
TURNED
UNDER

finishing

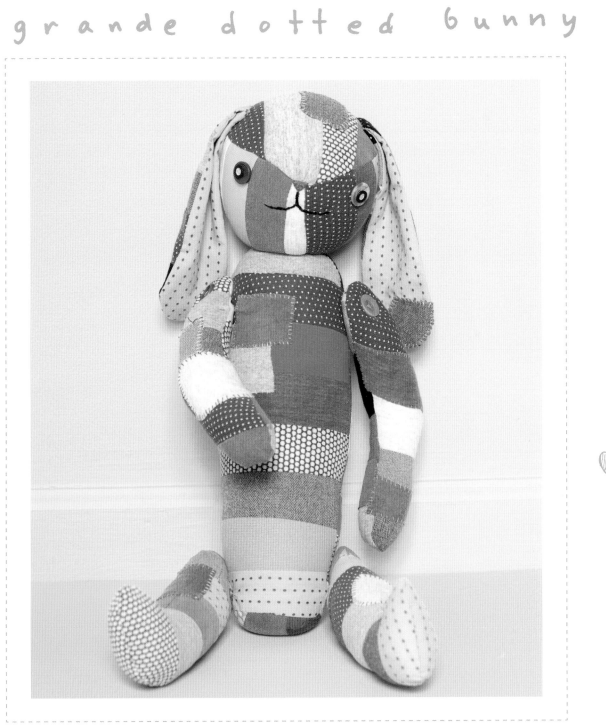

grande dotted bunny

For Grande Dotted Bunny, I accumulated a pile of dotted fabrics, then mixed them up with neutral grays, greens, and blues. Grande Dotted Bunny is similar to the Graffiti Bear, but the ear shape, head angle, posture, and color palette result in a unique look that is all his own.

MATERIALS

Patterns A–H (pages 91–92)

one 14" x 26" (35.5cm x 66cm) patchwork fabric piece (Creating Patchwork Fabric, page 13)

pins and washable fabric marker, if desired

scissors

sewing needle and thread

embroidery needle and thread

six ½" (13mm) buttons (for eyes, arms, and legs)

stuffing

iron (if needed)

INSTRUCTIONS

1 Fold the fabric lengthwise with right sides facing, then cut out and pin the paper patterns onto the fabric, noting the number of pieces for each. Match the orientation of the patchwork strips on the paper patterns to your fabric. Mark the X points, and cut out the patterns.

2 With right sides facing, sew together in pairs the body (B), arm (F), leg (A), and ear (G) pieces, leaving openings as shown in the assembly diagrams. Turn all sewn pieces right side out. Repair any patchwork seams that have come apart (page 14) using a small fell stitch, and trim seam allowances to ³⁄₁₆" (4.5mm).

3 With right sides facing, sew the head top piece (D) to a head piece (C), aligning and sewing from X point to X point from the crown to the nose as shown. Then, sew the opposite edge of the head top piece (D) to the remaining head piece (C). Sew along the front edge of the head piece (C) from nose to neck at X points.

4 With right sides facing, attach the head back piece (E) to the rest of the head. Begin sewing at the X points in the center of the sewn head pieces, and continue down each side of the head, leaving a neck opening. Turn the head right side out.

5 With right sides facing, attach the bottom piece (H) to the sewn body pieces (B) using a small running or machine stitch, aligning X points as shown. Work around as best as you can, then turn inside out and finish using a running stitch. When you have finished, turn right side out again.

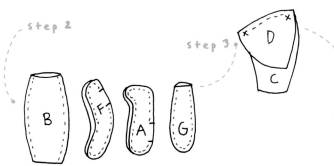

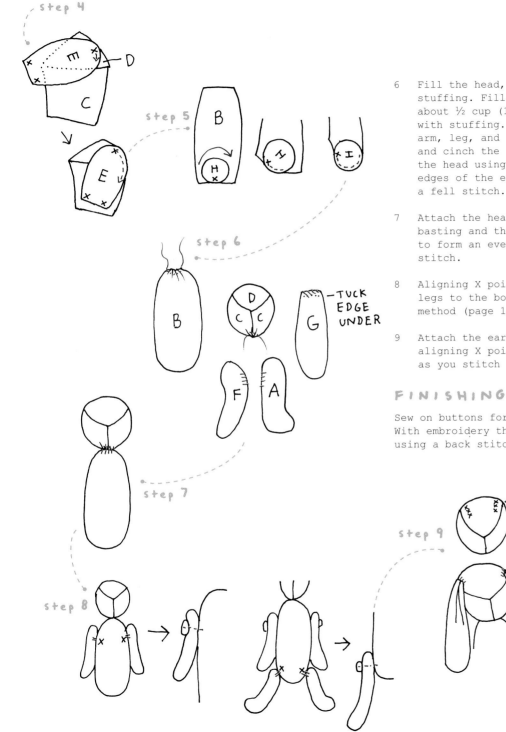

6 Fill the head, body, arms, and legs firmly with stuffing. Fill the bottom of the body first with about ½ cup (118mL) of weighted filler and then with stuffing. Do not stuff the ears. Close the arm, leg, and ear openings using a fell stitch, and cinch the top of the body and the base of the head using a gathering stitch. Turn the edges of the ears under, then sew the seam using a fell stitch.

7 Attach the head to the body as shown, lightly basting and then sewing around the seam again to form an even, strong attachment using a fell stitch.

8 Aligning X points as shown, attach the arms and legs to the body using the button attachment method (page 15).

9 Attach the ears to the head using a slip stitch, aligning X points and pinching the ears in half as you stitch as shown.

FINISHING

Sew on buttons for eyes according to the pattern. With embroidery thread, stitch a nose and mouth using a back stitch.

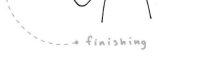

little fish

For Little Fish, I used fabric from three shirts: neutral blue and gray gingham for the body of the fish, and two dainty plaids for the head, tail, and fins. The three prints harmonize together, gridlike, creating an altogether very special fish.

MATERIALS

Patterns A-F (page 93)

two 6" x 6" (15cm x 15cm) fabric pieces (for fins and head)

two 8" x 8" (20.5cm x 20.5cm) fabric pieces (for body)

one 4" x 4" (10cm x 10cm) fabric piece (for side fins)

pins and washable fabric marker, if desired

scissors

sewing needle and thread

embroidery needle and thread

two ⅜" (9mm) buttons (for eyes)

rickrack (12" [30.5cm] long x ¼" [6mm] wide)

stuffing

iron (if needed)

INSTRUCTIONS

1   Cut out and pin the paper patterns onto the fabric, noting the number of pieces for each. Mark the X points, and cut the patterns in pairs, with right sides facing.

2   With right sides facing, align the X points and sew one body piece (A) to one head piece (B) along the short curved edges. Repeat with the remaining body (A) and head (B) pieces. Flip over both sewn pieces to lay flat.

3   With right sides facing, sew together in pairs the tail (C), top fin (D), side fin (E) (optional), and bottom fin (F) pieces, leaving the flat ends open. Trim the seam allowance to ³⁄₁₆" (4.5mm). Turn all fin pieces right side out and fill pieces lightly with stuffing.

4   Pin the tail and top and bottom fins to the right side of one of the body pieces, aligning X points of each tail or fin as indicated on the pattern. With right sides facing, pin the body pieces together. The fins and tail will be sandwiched in between these pieces as shown in the assembly diagram. Then, carefully sew the body pieces together in an even curve, leaving an opening between the bottom fin and the head, as marked.

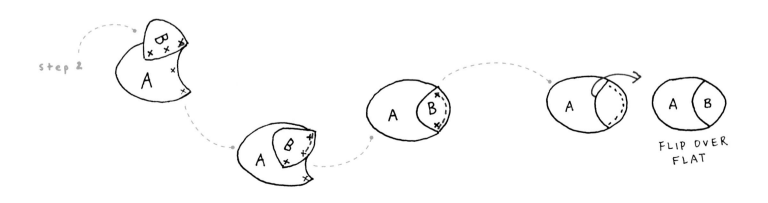

step 2

FLIP OVER FLAT

INSTRUCTIONS (cont.)

5 Turn the Fish right side out at the opening and firmly fill with stuffing to even out any bumps along the edges. Use a fell stitch to stitch the opening closed, tucking in edges.

FINISHING

Sew on buttons for eyes, referring to the pattern as a guide to placement.

With embroidery thread, hand-stitch details on the fins and the tail using a running stitch. Attach an 18" (45.5cm) loop of rickrack to the top fin for hanging. Use a fell stitch to attach optional side fins (E), if desired.

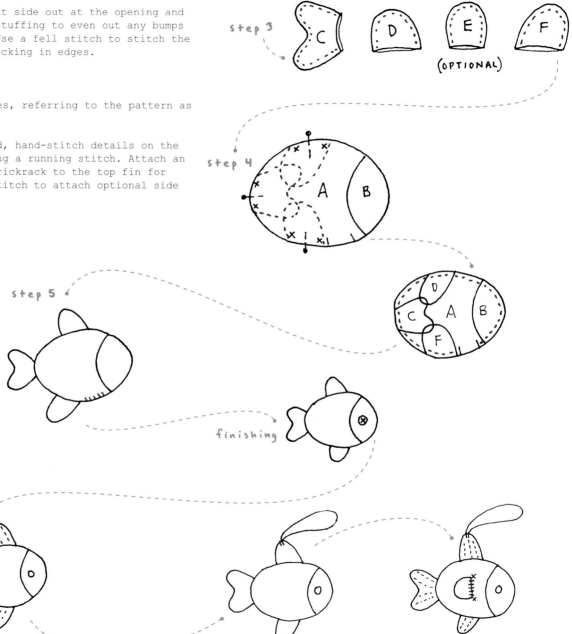

variation: piggy

mr. big head

Mr. Big Head wears a hat, pants, and a little shirt. I pieced together scraps from several men's plaid flannel shirts and a gray one, too, then strategically cut out the patterns so that Mr. Big Head would be well-dressed for any occasion.

MATERIALS

Patterns A, D-H (page 94)

one 12" x 15" (30.5cm x 38cm) patchwork fabric piece (for body, hands, legs, and ears, Creating Patchwork Fabric, page 13)

one 4" x 8" (10cm x 20.5cm) striped T-shirt fabric piece (for arms)

one 2" x 2" (5cm x 5cm) dark-colored felt piece (for eyes)

pins and washable fabric marker, if using

scissors

sewing needle and thread

embroidery needle and thread

stuffing

weighted filler and paper funnel

multipurpose glue or cement

iron

INSTRUCTIONS

1   Fold the patchwork fabric in half widthwise, with right sides facing. Iron flat. Cut out and pin paper patterns for body (A), hand (G), leg (E), ear (D) pieces onto the patchwork fabric, the arm piece (H) onto the T-shirt fabric, and the eye piece (F) onto the felt, noting the number of pieces for each. Mark the X points, and cut out the patterns.

2   With right sides facing, sew together in pairs the body (A), hand (G), leg (E), and ear (D) pieces, leaving openings as shown in the assembly diagram. Turn all parts right side out.

3   Roll arms (H) so that the stripes appear perpendicular to the length of the arm (each arm is made up of one piece) and sew closed with a fell stitch as shown.

4   Fill the body firmly with stuffing until about 2" (5cm) remain, then add weighted filler. Fill the legs mostly with weighted filler, then add a little stuffing in at the end. Fill the remaining parts with stuffing, and close with a fell stitch. Hand-stitch closed the hands and body using a gathering stitch.

5   Attach one end of an arm tube to a hand using a fell stitch, then attach the opposite end of the arm tube to the side of the body at the center X point using the flat-stitch attachment method (page 15). Attach the opposite hand and arm to the body in the same manner.

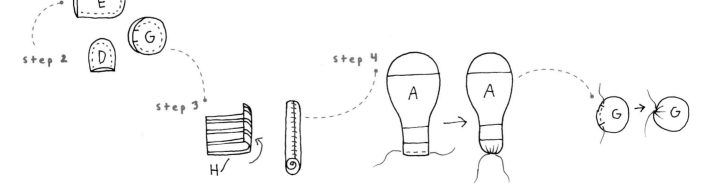

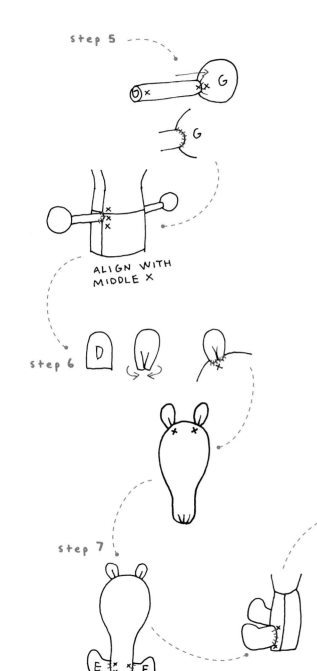

step 5

ALIGN WITH MIDDLE X

step 6

step 7

6 Attach the ears to the head using a slip stitch, aligning X points and pinching the ears in half as you stitch to form a U-shape as shown.

7 Turn under the edges of the legs ³⁄₁₆" (4.5mm), and stitch legs to the body using the flat-stitch attachment method (page 15) at X points slightly forward of the body's side seam as shown.

8 Glue on felt eyes (F) as indicated on the pattern template.

FINISHING

With embroidery thread, add a mouth using a knotless start (page 18) and one long 1" (2.5cm) stitch. End using the no-knot glue method (page 18).

★ Variations The shape of a toy doesn't have to be literal. Just look at Piggy (page 74). These two creatures may share the same body type, but they are anything but identical.

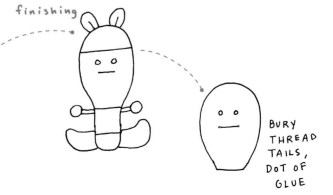

finishing

BURY THREAD TAILS, DOT OF GLUE

piggy

mr. big head variation

VARIATION MATERIALS

Patterns B, C, I-K (page 94) (Patterns D, F-H are not used.)

two 9" x 12" (23cm x 30.5cm) sweater pieces (for body, arms, legs, ears, and snout)

two 4" x 8" (10cm x 20.5cm) shirt pieces (for ears and tail)

one 4" x 4" (10cm x 10cm) sweater piece (for snout)

two ⅜" (9mm) buttons (for eyes)

two 6" (15cm) lengths of pipe cleaner

one 4" (10cm) length of pipe cleaner

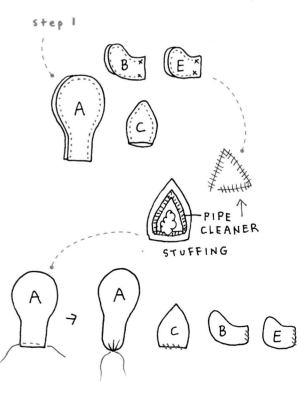

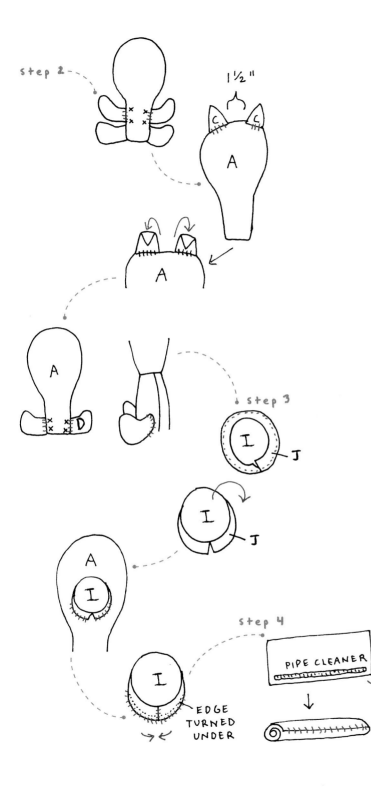

INSTRUCTIONS

1 Follow instructions for Mr. Big Head, sewing the ear pieces (C) from pairs of alternating fabrics, and arm pieces (B) together. Fill and sew closed all parts of the toy with stuffing, as for Mr. Big Head, except for the ears. Before stitching ears closed, bend the two 6" (15cm) lengths of pipe cleaner into triangle shapes and fit them into the contrasting ear pieces (C). Stitch closed, anchoring the pipe cleaner into the stitching.

2 Stitch the arms to the body using a fell stitch, aligning X points as shown, and the ears to the seam at the top of the head so that the patterned fabric faces the front of the toy. Continue following the instructions for Mr. Big Head, attaching the legs to the toy.

3 With right sides facing, stitch the snout edge piece (J) around the snout piece (I) using a small running stitch or small machine stitch as shown. Turn the edge out and carefully stitch the snout onto the face using a slip stitch, turning under the unsewn edges 3/16" (4.5mm) as you stitch. Add stuffing to the snout before completing the stitching.

4 To make the tail, lay the 4" (10cm) length of pipe cleaner along the edge of the tail piece (K). Roll up the pipe cleaner in the fabric, and stitch closed along the fabric edge using a fell stitch. Twist the tail around your finger to curl. Attach the tail to the back of the toy using a fell stitch as shown.

FINISHING

Sew on button eyes, and with embroidery thread, stitch nostrils and eyelashes using a back stitch as shown. Hide the ends by using the burying the tails method (page 19).

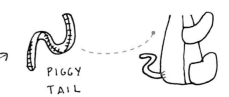

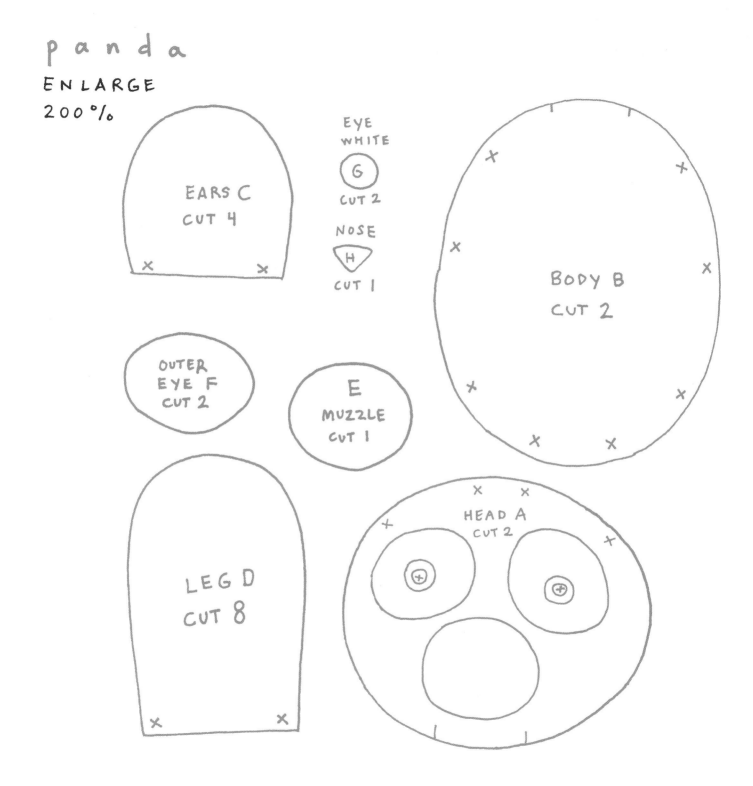

panda

ENLARGE
200%

EARS C
CUT 4

EYE
WHITE
G
CUT 2

NOSE
H
CUT 1

BODY B
CUT 2

OUTER
EYE F
CUT 2

E
MUZZLE
CUT 1

LEG D
CUT 8

HEAD A
CUT 2

houndstooth pup

ENLARGE
190%

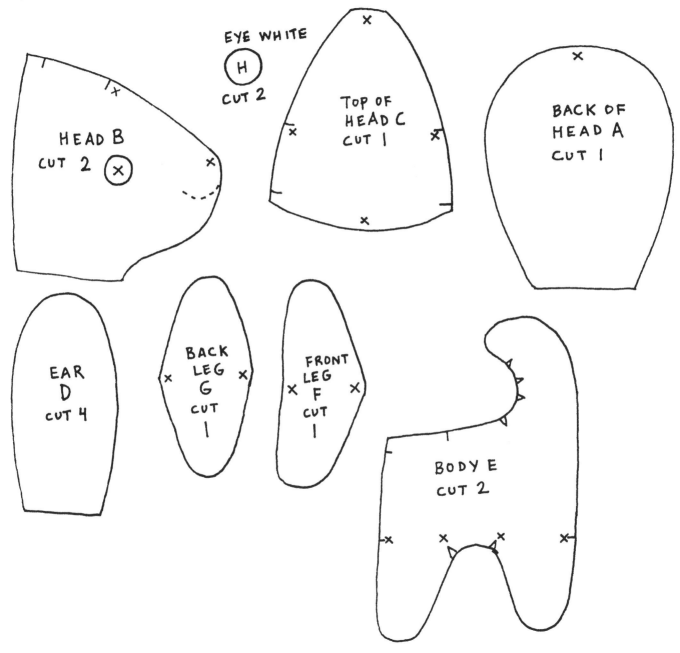

EYE WHITE
H
CUT 2

TOP OF
HEAD C
CUT 1

BACK OF
HEAD A
CUT 1

HEAD B
CUT 2

EAR
D
CUT 4

BACK
LEG
G
CUT
1

FRONT
LEG
F
CUT
1

BODY E
CUT 2

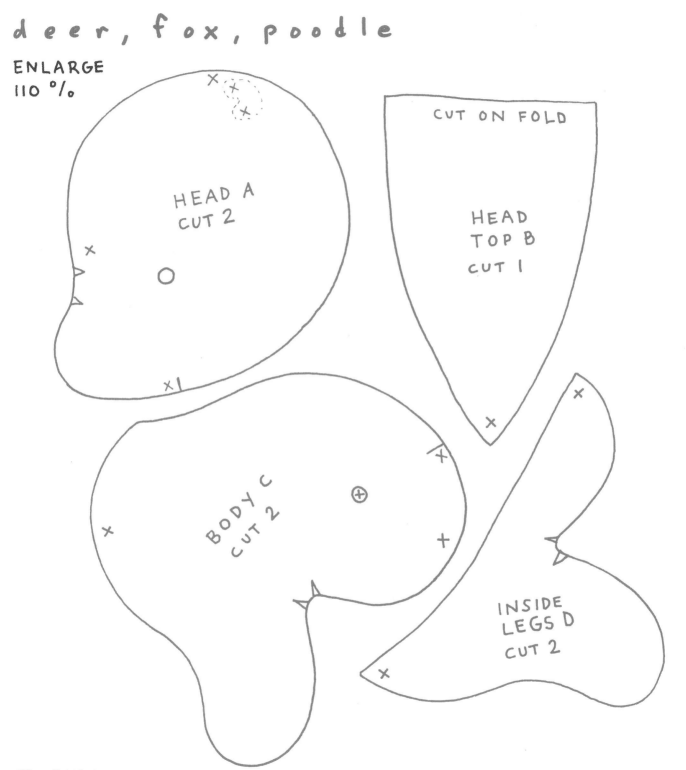

deer, fox, poodle

ENLARGE
110 %

HEAD A
CUT 2

CUT ON FOLD

HEAD
TOP B
CUT 1

BODY C
CUT 2

INSIDE
LEGS D
CUT 2

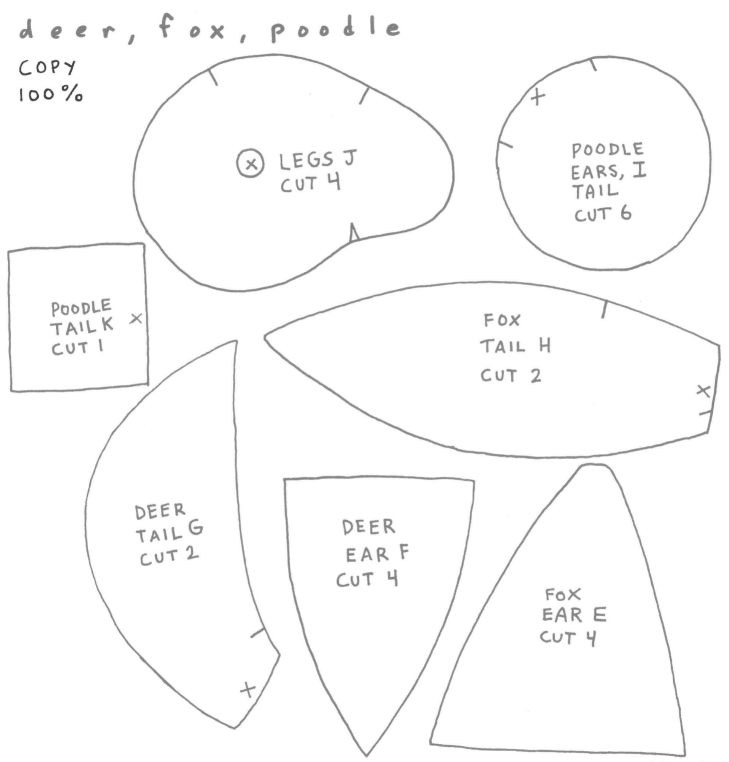

deer, fox, poodle

COPY
100%

LEGS J
CUT 4

POODLE
EARS, I
TAIL
CUT 6

POODLE
TAIL K
CUT 1

FOX
TAIL H
CUT 2

DEER
TAIL G
CUT 2

DEER
EAR F
CUT 4

FOX
EAR E
CUT 4

lazy kitty

ENLARGE
200 %

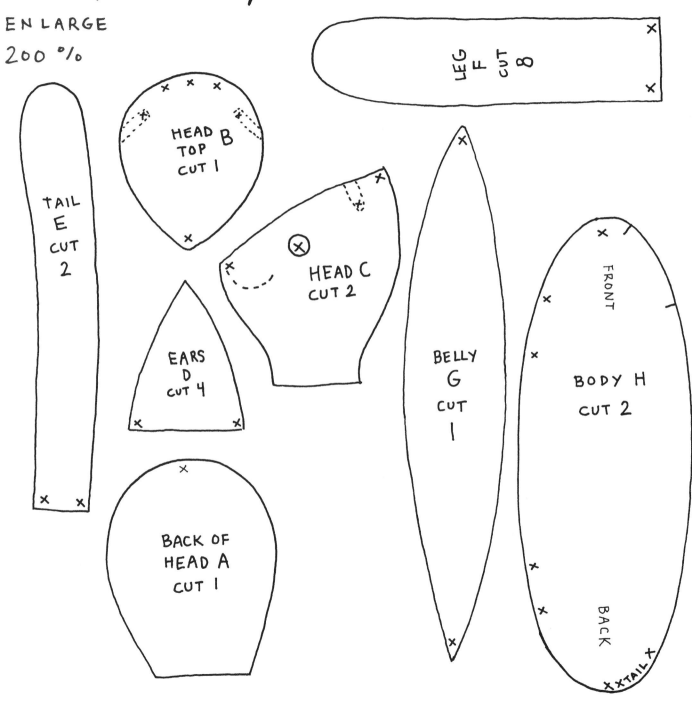

LEG F CUT 8

HEAD TOP B CUT 1

TAIL E CUT 2

HEAD C CUT 2

EARS D CUT 4

BELLY G CUT 1

BODY H CUT 2

FRONT

BACK

TAIL

BACK OF HEAD A CUT 1

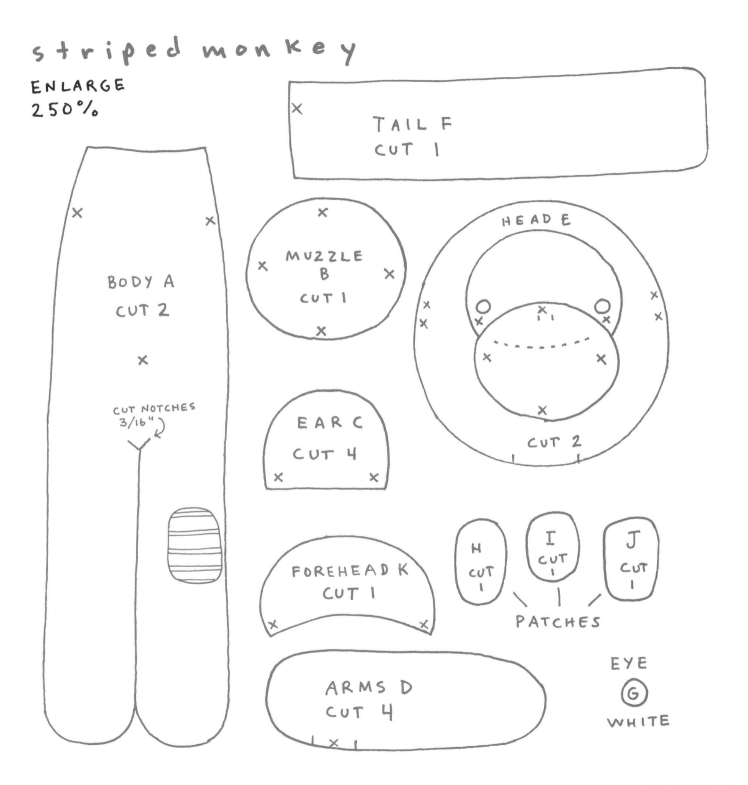

striped monkey

ENLARGE
250%

TAIL F
CUT 1

BODY A
CUT 2

CUT NOTCHES
3/16"

MUZZLE
B
CUT 1

EAR C
CUT 4

HEAD E

CUT 2

FOREHEAD K
CUT 1

H
CUT
1

I
CUT
1

J
CUT
1

PATCHES

ARMS D
CUT 4

EYE
G
WHITE

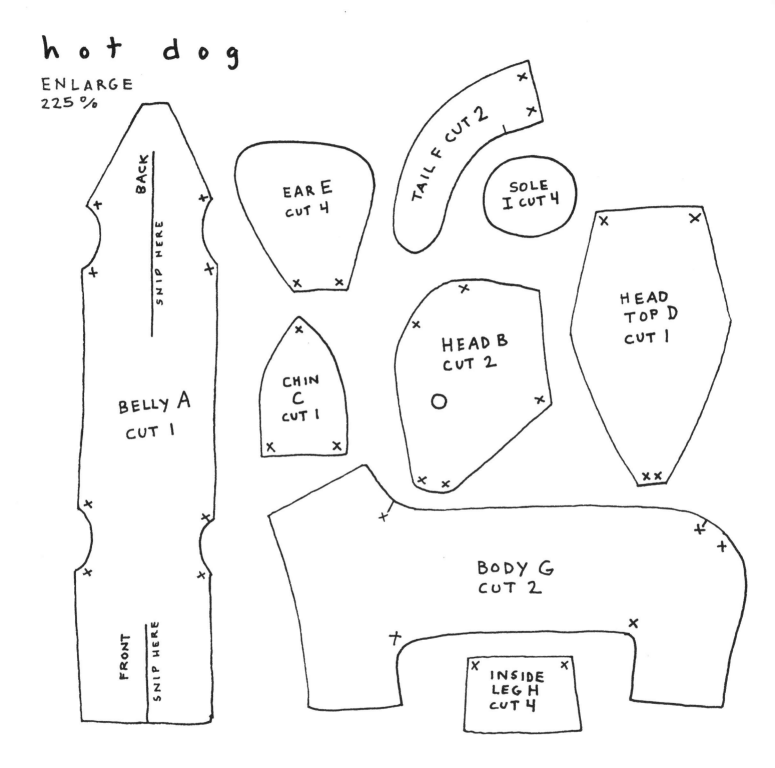

hot dog

ENLARGE
225 %

BACK
SNIP HERE

BELLY A
CUT 1

FRONT
SNIP HERE

EAR E
CUT 4

CHIN
C
CUT 1

TAIL F CUT 2

SOLE
I CUT 4

HEAD B
CUT 2

HEAD
TOP D
CUT 1

BODY G
CUT 2

INSIDE
LEG H
CUT 4

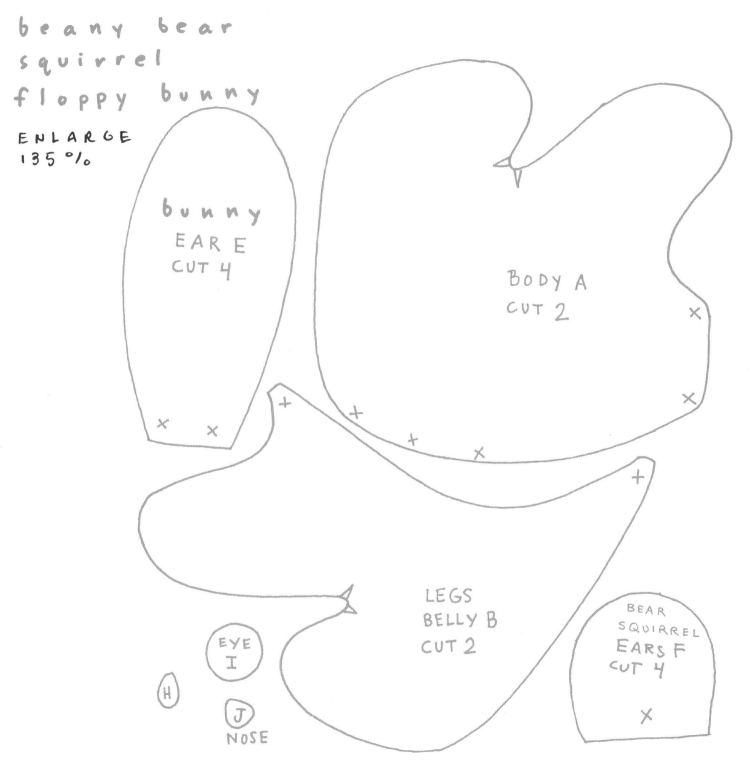

beany bear
squirrel
floppy bunny

ENLARGE
135%

bunny
EAR E
CUT 4

BODY A
CUT 2

LEGS
BELLY B
CUT 2

BEAR
SQUIRREL
EARS F
CUT 4

EYE
I

H

J
NOSE

beany bear
squirrel
floppy bunny

COPY
100%

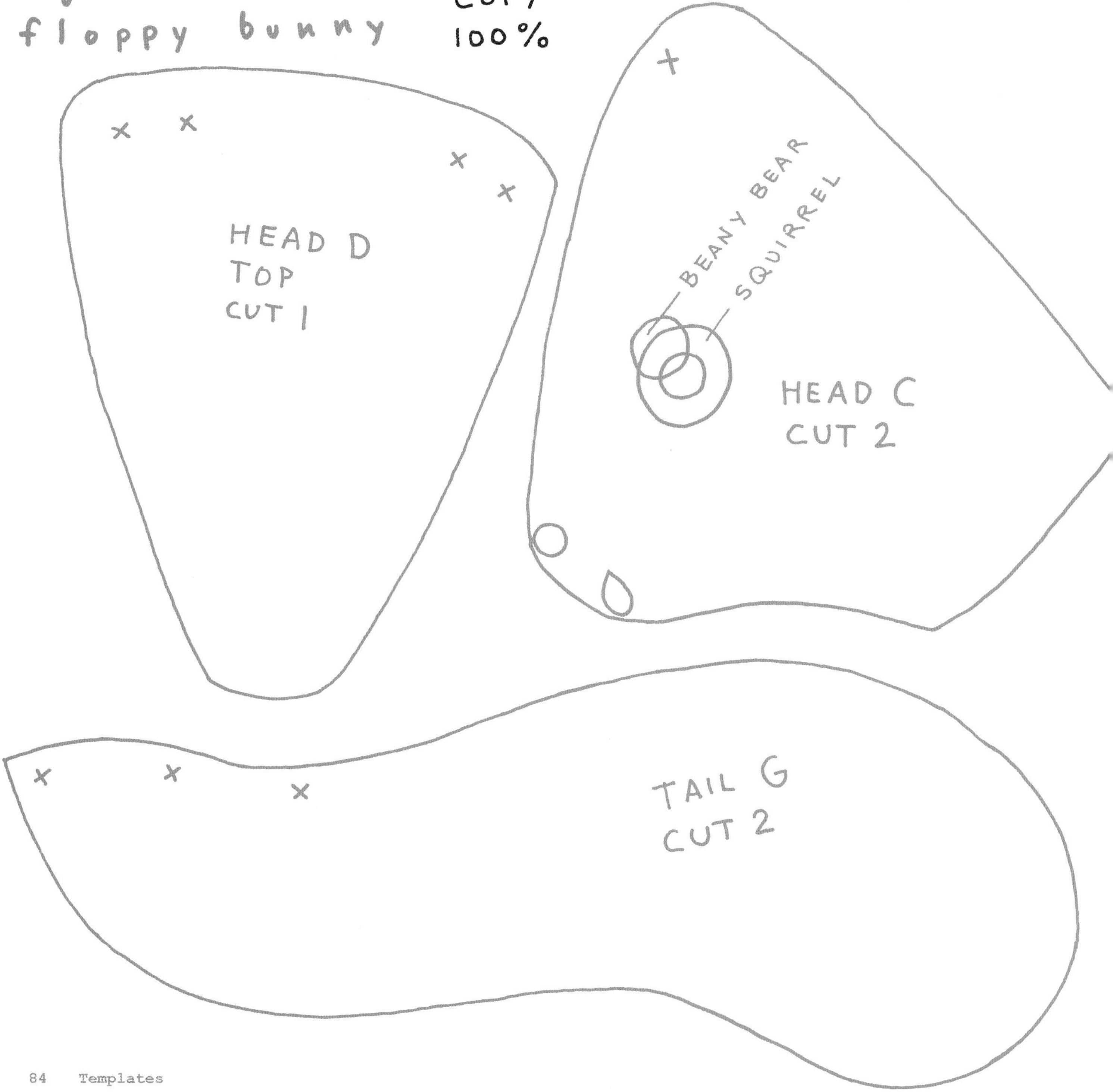

X   X

X
X

HEAD D
TOP
CUT 1

X

BEANY BEAR

SQUIRREL

HEAD C
CUT 2

X   X   X

TAIL G
CUT 2

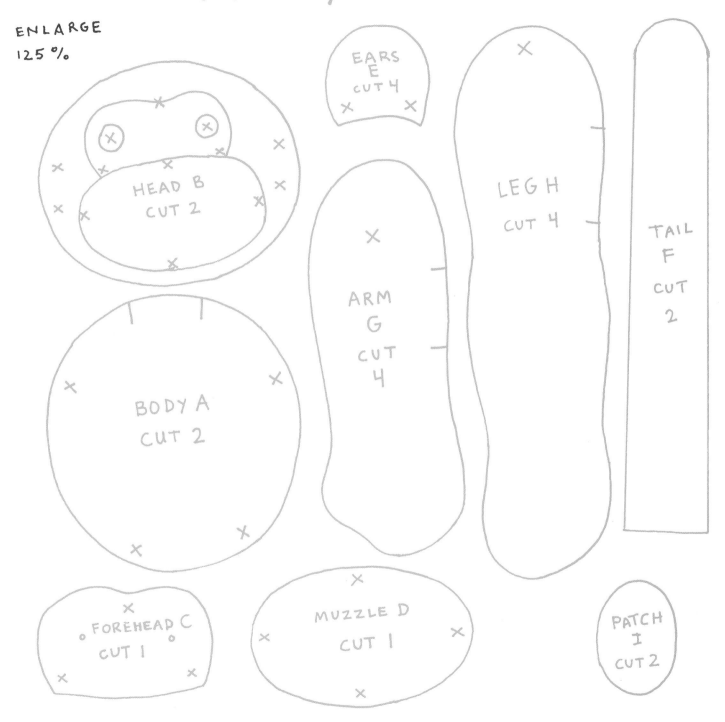

mini monkey

ENLARGE
125%

HEAD B
CUT 2

EARS
E
CUT 4

LEG H
CUT 4

TAIL
F
CUT
2

ARM
G
CUT
4

BODY A
CUT 2

FOREHEAD C
CUT 1

MUZZLE D
CUT 1

PATCH
I
CUT 2

elephant

ENLARGE
140%

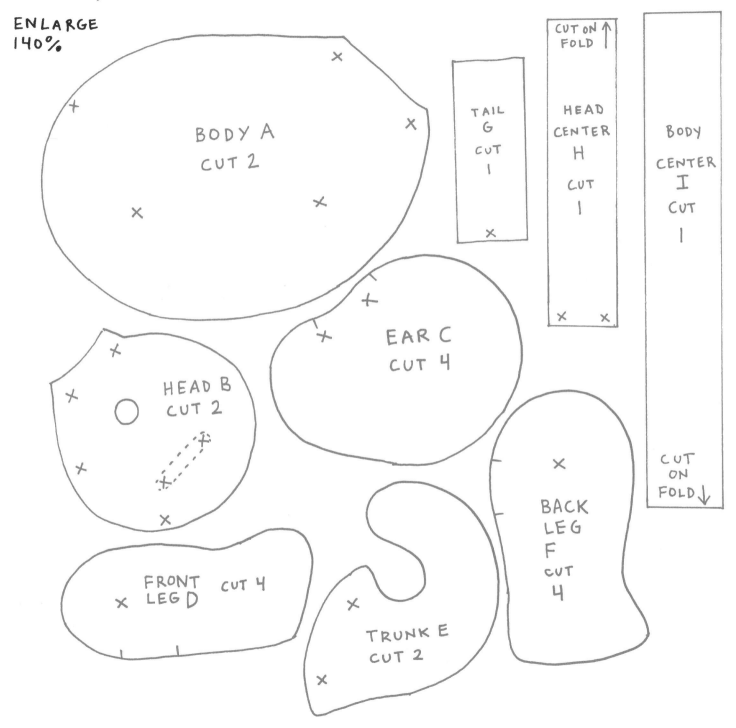

BODY A
CUT 2

TAIL
G
CUT
1

CUT ON
FOLD ↑

HEAD
CENTER
H
CUT
1

BODY
CENTER
I
CUT
1

HEAD B
CUT 2

EAR C
CUT 4

CUT
ON
FOLD ↓

BACK
LEG
F
CUT
4

FRONT
LEG D   CUT 4

TRUNK E
CUT 2

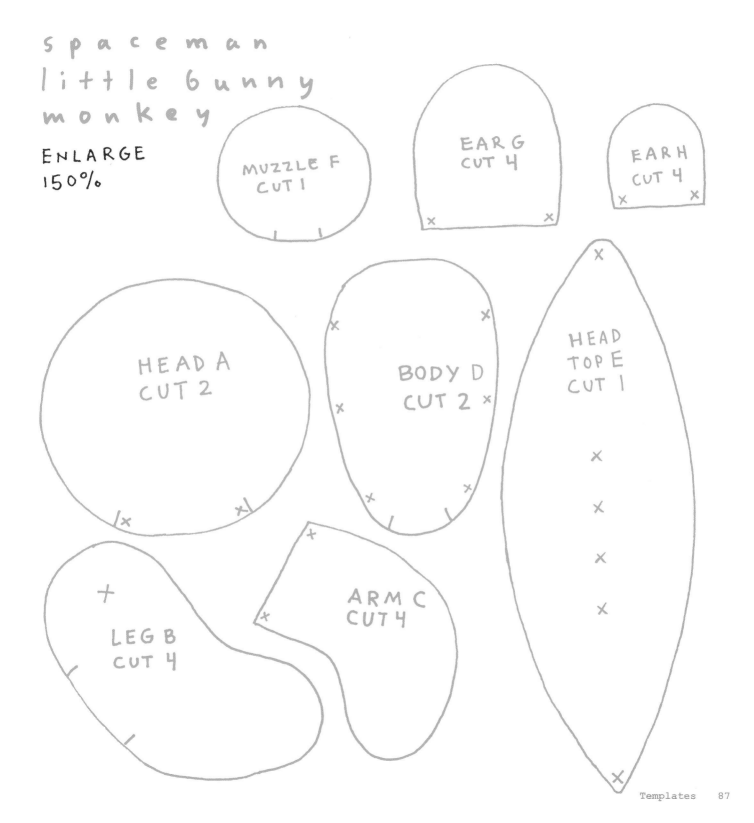

spaceman
little bunny
monkey

ENLARGE
150%

MUZZLE F
CUT 1

EAR G
CUT 4

EAR H
CUT 4

HEAD A
CUT 2

BODY D
CUT 2

HEAD
TOP E
CUT 1

LEG B
CUT 4

ARM C
CUT 4

penguin

ENLARGE
185%

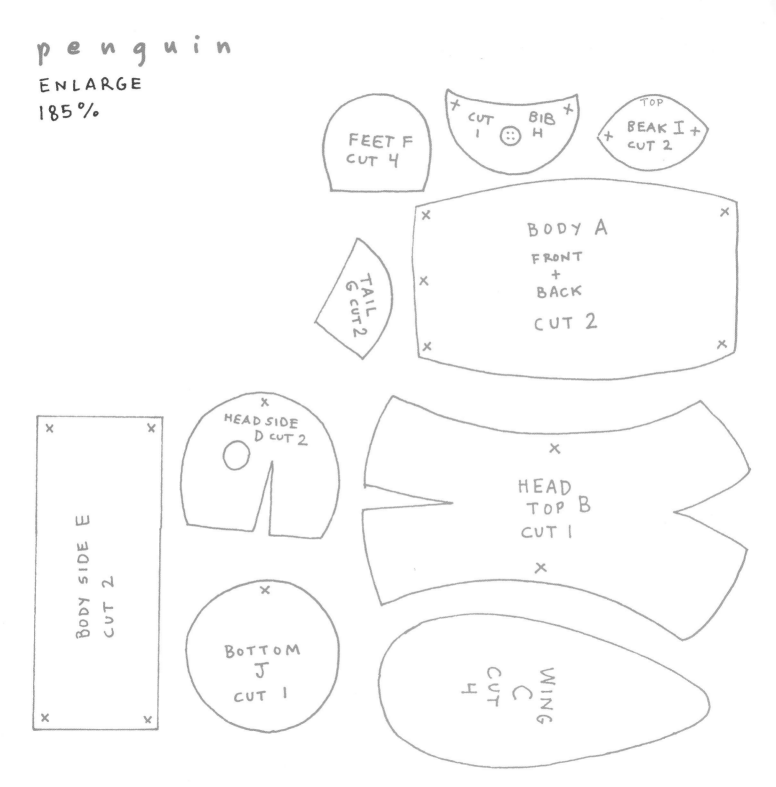

FEET F
CUT 4

CUT 1   BIB H

TOP
BEAK I
CUT 2

BODY A

FRONT
+
BACK

CUT 2

TAIL
G CUT 2

HEAD SIDE
D CUT 2

HEAD
TOP B
CUT 1

BODY SIDE E
CUT 2

BOTTOM
J
CUT 1

WING
C
CUT
4

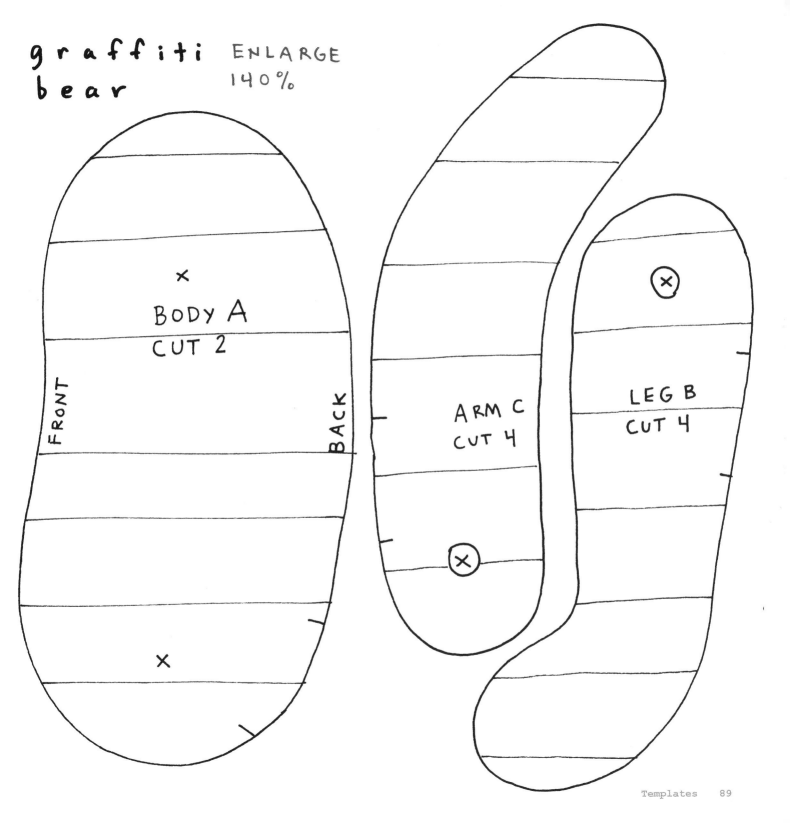

graffiti bear ENLARGE 140%

BODY A
CUT 2

FRONT

BACK

ARM C
CUT 4

LEG B
CUT 4

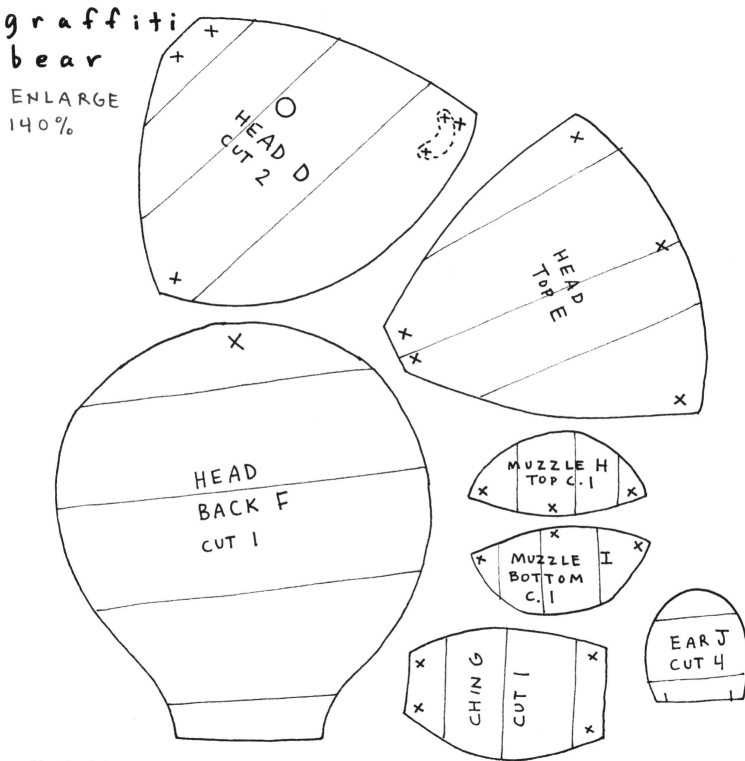

graffiti
bear

ENLARGE
140%

HEAD D
CUT 2

HEAD
TOP E

HEAD
BACK F
CUT 1

MUZZLE H
TOP C.1

MUZZLE I
BOTTOM
C.1

CHIN G
CUT 1

EAR J
CUT 4

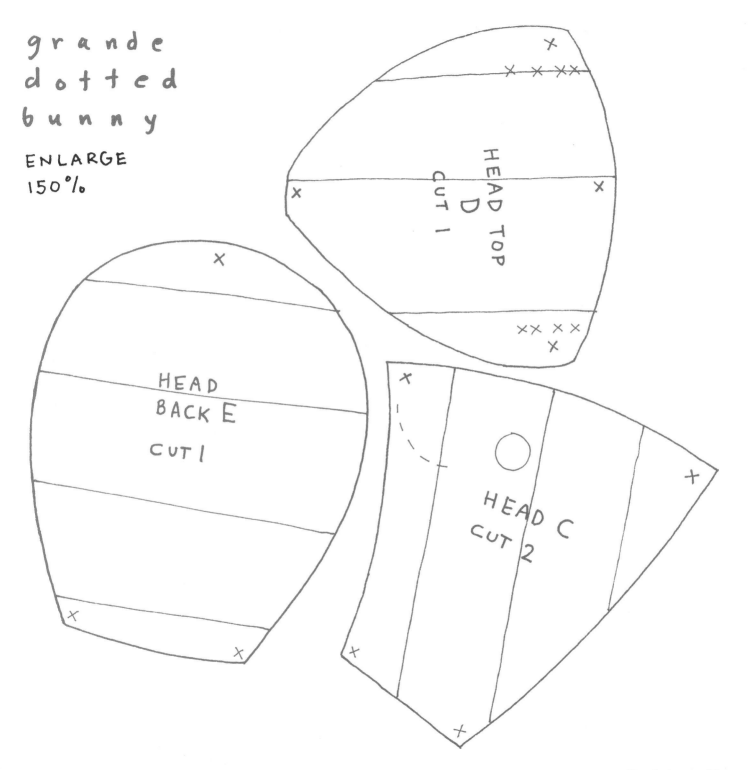

grande
dotted
bunny

ENLARGE
150%

HEAD TOP
D
CUT 1

HEAD
BACK E

CUT 1

HEAD C
CUT 2

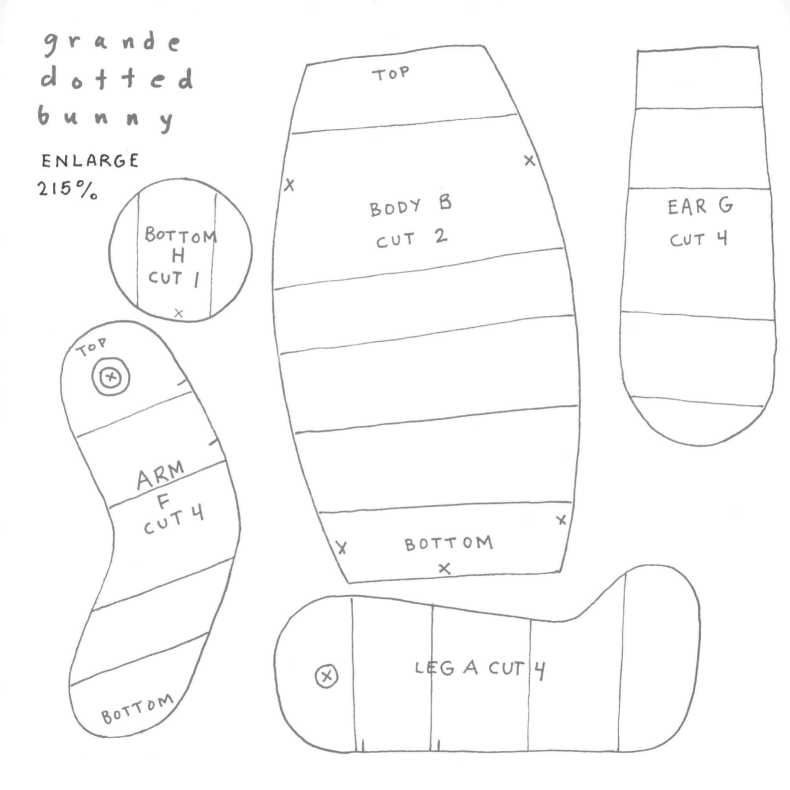

grande
dotted
bunny

ENLARGE
215%

BOTTOM
H
CUT 1

TOP

BODY B
CUT 2

BOTTOM

EAR G
CUT 4

TOP

ARM
F
CUT 4

BOTTOM

LEG A CUT 4

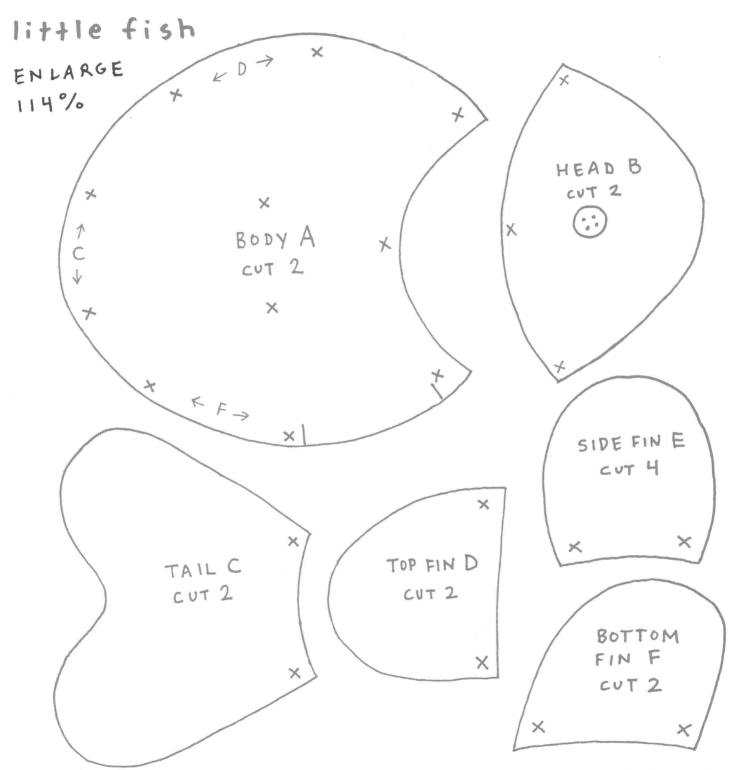

little fish

ENLARGE 114%

BODY A
CUT 2

HEAD B
CUT 2

TAIL C
CUT 2

TOP FIN D
CUT 2

SIDE FIN E
CUT 4

BOTTOM
FIN F
CUT 2

mr. big head, piggy

ENLARGE
190 %

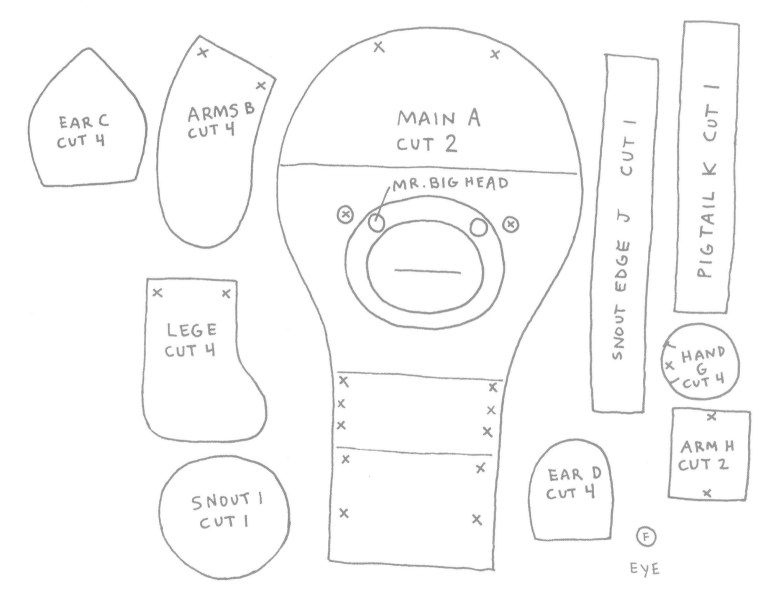

WE USED TO PLAY A GAME—WHO COULD DRAW
THE MEANEST-LOOKING CHARACTERS.

I'D LOSE BECAUSE MINE ALWAYS CAME OUT
TOO CUTE.

FOR BILL, WHO UNDERSTOOD MY PARTICULAR
VERSION OF FUNNY, WEIRD, AND CUTE.

ACKNOWLEDGMENTS

Thanks to each and every one of my friends and family who
have been supportive of my work over the years. Thanks to
my pal Ida Pearle; whenever I finish a project, I think,
"*IDA* might like this!!" Special thanks to little Emmet
and Augie for trying out my first Little Fish, and to my
students at Pratt for testing my patterns. Thanks to Adam
Reed for his support, for putting up with my messes, and
especially for Piggy's tail. Thanks to my mom and dad—
both serious crafters who love to make things with their
hands—for all of their encouragement and for bringing us
up on the farm, the beautiful place that set the scene
for my earliest "crafting." Thanks to Heather Weston for
the beautiful photographs. Thanks also to Josh Jordon for
noticing my work, to Karrie Witkin at Potter Style; and
to Thom O'Hearn, Rebecca Behan, La Tricia Watford, and
the rest of the team at Potter Craft for their excellent,
careful guidance in shaping this book.

RESOURCES

Even though I sew all the time, I hardly ever go to the
craft store. I tend to find my fabrics in thrift stores or
in my own closet—there are always old clothes around! In
a pinch, most drug stores carry standard threads and packs
of assorted needles, though of course the selection isn't
anywhere near as good as at a specialty store.

If you do take a trip to your local craft store or one of
the big chains, there's plenty to stock up on. In addition
to standard needles and thread, pick up embroidery needles
and thread, a big bag of stuffing, rickrack, fabric glue and
markers, and any felt or fabric that looks toy-worthy. You
may be able to buy some buttons as well, but I think it's
more fun to find bags of assorted buttons at online auction
websites like eBay or in thrift stores or antique shops—or
simply snip them off of clothing you no longer wear.

INDEX

Numbers in italics indicate templates.

Published in the United States by Potter Craft, an imprint of the Crown Publishing Group, a division of Random House, Inc., New York.
www.crownpublishing.com
www.pottercraft.com

POTTER CRAFT and colophon is a registered trademark of Random House, Inc.

Library of Congress Cataloging-in-Publication Data
Havens, Sue.

  Make your own toys : sew soft bears, bunnies, monkeys, puppies, and more! / Sue Havens.
    p. cm.
  Includes index.
  ISBN 978-0-307-58644-5
  1. Soft toy making. I. Title.
TT174.3.H48 2010
745.592'4--dc22

2009050118

Printed in China

Design by La Tricia Watford
Photography by Heather Weston

10 9 8 7 6 5 4 3 2 1

First Edition